CACHE LEVEL

2

Award in Child Development and Care

◆ Penny Tassoni
◆ Louise Burnham

HODDER
EDUCATION
AN HACHETTE UK COMPANY

The Authors and Publishers would like to thank the following for permission to reproduce copyright material.

Every effort has been made to trace all copyright holders, but if any have been inadvertently overlooked, the Publishers will be pleased to make the necessary arrangements at the first opportunity.

Although every effort has been made to ensure that website addresses are correct at time of going to press, Hodder Education cannot be held responsible for the content of any website mentioned in this book. It is sometimes possible to find a relocated web page by typing in the address of the home page for a website in the URL window of your browser.

Hachette UK's policy is to use papers that are natural, renewable and recyclable products and made from wood grown in sustainable forests. The logging and manufacturing processes are expected to conform to the environmental regulations of the country of origin.

Orders: please contact Bookpoint Ltd, 130 Park Drive, Milton Park, Abingdon, Oxon OX14 4SE. Telephone: (44) 01235 827720. Fax: (44) 01235 400454. Email education@bookpoint.co.uk Lines are open from 9 a.m.to 5 p.m., Monday to Saturday, with a 24-hour message answering service. You can also order through our website: www.hoddereducation.co.uk

ISBN: 9781510416529

First published in 2017 by

Hodder Education,

An Hachette UK Company

Carmelite House

50 Victoria Embankment

London EC4Y 0DZ

www.hoddereducation.co.uk

Impression number   10 9 8 7 6 5 4 3 2 1

Year   2020 2019 2018 2017

Cover photo: © AnaBGD / iStockphoto

Illustrations by Aptara Inc.

Typeset in India

Printed in Italy

A catalogue record for this title is available from the British Library.

CONTENTS

■ How to use this book

Key features of the book

High priority

Make sure that you know what is meant by an early years setting.

Early years setting – an early years group where children's learning and development is nurtured by adults.

The most important things to focus on

Jargon buster

Ofsted (Office for Standards in Education, Children's Services and Skills) – Ofsted is a government organisation which exists to monitor and inspect different types of services that care for children and young people and provide education and skills for learners of all ages.

Understand the meaning of important terms

Theory in action

A new family have recently moved house with three children aged three months, two years and four years. Both parents work: the father full time and the mother for three days a week. What different types of childcare setting might they find useful for their regular childcare, and why?

Real-life situations that show how theory links to practice

My life as a childminder

My name is Sinead and I have worked as a registered childminder for four years. It has been great for me and I have done it as my own children have grown older and the eldest has started school. I used to work in a nursery before having children but I find that childminding suits me better at this stage; I may go back to working in a larger setting and gain more childcare qualifications when my own children are all at school full time. As a childminder, I like the fact that young children are being cared for in a home environment, and I feel that I have closer relationships with parents and children.

Finding out the roles of different early years professionals

Find out more about ...

... the entitlements to free childcare for children in England which is issued by the Department for Education (DfE)

Tasks that involve further reading or research

Activity

Choose a childcare setting in your local area and look at the information which is available on their website. How is the information organised?

Practical tasks to support your learning

Read and write

Both the 'Find out more about ...' and the 'Top marks' tasks ask you to write down what you can about different settings in your local area. You will need to research and read about this by looking locally, through using your local library or children's centre, for what is available in your area. You might also look online at your local Children's Information Service or local authority website.

Tasks to help your literacy skills

Top marks

For this unit's assignment, you need to show that you can reflect on the role of the early years worker when meeting the individual needs of children aged 0–5 years.

List the requirements of the role of the early years worker when meeting the individual needs of children, saying why each one is important and giving examples of what might happen if it is not met effectively by staff.

What to focus on in order to gain the highest grades

Grading

To achieve these assessment criteria you will need to:

D2 Identify settings within local provision from across the sectors.

A1 Discuss the differences between types of provision available for children aged 0–5 years

What is needed to achieve different grading criteria

Five things to know when preparing for placement

1) Carefully research the settings which are available for your placement.
2) Make sure you always communicate clearly and politely with your placement co-ordinator.
3) Know the name of the person you are going to meet and make sure you have contacted and visited them before you start your placement.
4) Always arrive on time or a little early if possible on placement days.
5) Inform the placement as soon as you can if you are unable to go in.

Essential points within a section

Extend

Think about other ways in which you could show employers that you are committed to your placement.

Increase your depth of knowledge

Check what you know

Make a checklist using bullet points that you can use to help you when you are preparing to start a placement in an early years setting.

Making sure that you can remember key points

Test yourself

To check that you know the types of movements, give two examples of:

- a fine motor movement
- a gross motor movement.

Opportunities for bite-sized revision

Test time

See if you can answer the following questions:

1 An early years worker is most likely to use an event sample to understand a child's
   a) Friendships
   b) Physical development
   c) Unwanted behaviour
   d) Language development

A chance to practise multiple choice questions

■ Introduction

I am delighted to write the foreword for this textbook which supports the increasingly popular Level 2 Award in Child Development and Care. This level 2 qualification provides the appropriate depth and breadth of knowledge necessary to introduce you to working effectively with young children.

The qualification contains three mandatory units. Mandatory means that you have to complete all three units identified here. These mandatory units are:
- Unit 1: An introduction to working with children aged 0–5 years
- Unit 2: Development and well-being 0–5 years
- Unit 3: Childcare and development 0–5 years

Units 1 and 2 are internally marked and graded by your tutor, while unit 3 is a synoptic assessment accessed via a Multiple Choice Question Paper and therefore externally set and externally marked.

This means that you will study each of the three units: for units 1 and 2 you will produce work for your tutor to mark, whereas for unit 3 you will study with your tutor and then you will take a Multiple Choice Question Paper. Synoptic means that the questions you will find on the Multiple Choice Question Paper test your knowledge and understanding of all three units.

The qualification, designed to be studied by learners from the age of 14 helps you to study for this qualification whilst also undertaking other subject areas at school for example.

As you work your way through the course the new learning that you receive will provide a firm foundation from which you can begin to make connections for future progression as well as helping you to make well-informed decisions about your career goals and aspirations.

This supportive textbook brings the specification alive, enlightening you with accurate, up to date and relevant practice, interesting examples and thought provoking case studies. These will help you to make sense of learning outcomes and assessment criteria. Great effort has been made to ensure that the content underpins the necessary learning to support you to do well. There are opportunities within the textbook to check your own learning and understanding and this provides an ideal base from which to prepare for your Multiple Choice Question Paper.

The textbook is arranged to allow you to find the information that you need easily and the text is incredibly user-friendly, enhanced by illustrations and short chunks of writing to appeal to everyone.

You are about to begin to learn about what is involved when caring for children 0-5 years of age, it is a fascinating and critically important area, enjoy your studies and good luck!

Janet King

CACHE Senior Subject Specialist

■ Acknowledgements

The authors would like to thank Janet King at CACHE for her valuable comments and contributions to this book as well as the team at Hodder Education, led by Stephen Halder, for their continued support. Both authors would also like to thank the many individuals and early years settings that over the years have provided them with ideas and inspiration.

Upon successful completion of this qualification, learners will be awarded the NCFE CACHE Level 2 Award in Child Development and Care (QRN: 600/6644/1). This CACHE branded qualification is certified by the Awarding Organisation, NCFE.

■ Photo Credits

The authors and publishers would like to thank the following for the use of photographs in the book.

Page1 Monika Olszewska – Fotolia; pages 5, 26, 29, 35, 41, 72, 165, 168, 185, 189, 195 © Andrew O'Callaghan/Hodder Education; pages 10, 11, 14, 19, 27, 33, 37, 46, 49, 52, 56, 62, 77, 104, 127, 145 top right, 159, 176, 193 © Jules Selmes/Hodder Education; page 54 Pavla Zakova – Fotolia; pages 58 © caia image/Alamy Stock Photo; page 64 and 151 © Firma V – Fotolia; page 65 © auremar – Fotolia; page 66 © Catchlight Visual Services/Alamy Stock Photo; page 68 © gpointstudio/Shutterstock; page 69 © naumenke/123RF; page 75 © d13/Shutterstock; page 79 © Susan MacLeod/Alamy Stock Photo; page 81 © Cebas/Shutterstock; page 107 © DenisNata/Shutterstock; page 112 © amVeld/Shutterstock; page 118 © matka_Wariatka/Shutterstock; page 120 © Satyrenko/Shutterstock; page 120 bottom © Sandra Peek/ Shutterstock; page 135 Andrey Kuzmin – Fotolia; page 139 © Tamas Vargyasi – Fotolia; page 141 © Nolte Lourens/Shutterstock; page 145 top left © Emilia Kun/Shutterstock; page 145 bottom left © Leila Cutler/Alamy Stock Photo; page 145 bottom right © Felix Mizioznikov/Shutterstock; page 176 © Kiselev Andrey Valerevich/Shutterstock; page 178 © Kzenon/Shutterstock; page 185, top © Andrey_Kuzmin/Shutterstock; page 199 © digitalskillet/Shutterstock.

Unit 1

An introduction to working with children aged 0–5 years

About this unit

This unit will give you an introduction to working with young children from 0–5 years. It is about the different kinds of childcare settings which are available and which you will need to know about if you are thinking of working with children. It also gives you information about how to prepare for a placement in a childcare setting through looking at issues such as dress code, timekeeping and working with others, as well as the kinds of responsibilities that early years workers have. You will also look at individual needs of children and the importance of fairness and inclusive practice. Finally, the unit will encourage you to think about your own preferred way of learning and the study skills that may be useful for you as you work your way through this qualification.

■ Learning Outcome 1: Understand the types of settings and local provision for children

Assessment criteria grid

Learning outcomes The learner will:	Assessment criteria The learner can:
1. Understand types of settings and local provision for children.	1.1. Describe the main types of settings available for children.
	1.2. Identify some of these settings within local provision.

High priority

Make sure that you know what is meant by an early years setting.

Early years setting – an early years group where children's learning and development are nurtured by adults.

Have you ever tried to list all the different types of childcare and early years settings which are on offer to parents? There are many kinds and they may be run in different ways, from a church hall at the end of the road to a large private nursery chain which has several different branches around the country. If you are going to be working with young children, you will need to know about and understand the differences between what is available. This chapter is about the main types of setting which provide childcare and education for young children and the provision which may be available in your area.

1.1 Describe the main types of settings available for children (D1 C1)

Early years settings may be funded and run by local authorities, voluntary organisations or private companies, and offer a range of different childcare approaches. Some may be small and run by charities and voluntary organisations, while others may be private and part of a national chain which is run for profit. As you start to think about a career in working with children, you may find the amount of different settings confusing. Make sure you know and understand what is available so that you are aware of some of the differences as well as what these settings have in common.

Early years settings may or may not need to be registered and inspected by Ofsted, depending on how they are run and staffed.

Types of childcare settings

Type of setting	Description	Age of children
Registered childminder	A registered childminder looks after the child in their home and is self-employed. They need to be registered and inspected by Ofsted, and offer flexible and individualised care for children. They can look after up to six children between the ages of birth to eight years, including their own.	0–8 years and above
School-based nursery	A school-based nursery will be attached to an infant or primary school and will usually be for children who are expected to move on to that school. They will only run during term time. The age at which they take children will vary according to the school and type of provision, but may start from two years in an independent school. However, a school-based nursery usually starts the year before a child begins full time education in Reception, so around four years.	Varies, but may be from two years
Reception class	A school Reception class will start during the year of the child's 5th birthday. Children may start by attending on a half-day basis but will quickly build up to a full day. School-based settings are registered and inspected by Ofsted.	4–5 years
Children's centres	Children's centres offer a range of different services for children aged under five and their families. They may be located on school sites through extended schools or based in local authority accommodation. These services may vary between different areas but may include health and support for families with young children. They also usually include play centres where parents can attend with their children on any day and time which is available.	0–5 years
Day nursery	A day nursery must be registered and inspected by Ofsted and is usually open all day. There may be different types of provision, for example private, voluntary and workplace based. Some will have longer hours and will be open during evenings and weekends.	0–5 years
Out of school clubs and play centres	These are clubs which are run for school-age children before and after school, and may run during school holidays.	4+
Parent and toddler group	These are drop-in sessions for parents of young children and are usually run by volunteers and other parents. Parents will have responsibility for their children.	0–3 years
Playgroup/ pre-school	A playgroup or pre-school may be run by parents or children may be left in the care of staff. If children are left in the care of staff, the pre-school must be registered with Ofsted. They are usually run on a voluntary basis during term time and have sessions of around three hours.	2–5 years
Workplace nursery	This provides care and education for children at the place where their parents work.	3 months and over
Nanny/home carer	A nanny is a carer who is employed by a child's parents to look after the child in their own home. Nannies will often look after more than one child if needed and are usually very flexible. However, although many do have training, they are not required to have qualifications.	0–5 years and over
Crèche	A crèche will provide interim care for children from time to time while their parents are engaged in a one-off activity such as shopping, sport, or other activity, usually on the same premises. They are not required to register with Ofsted but can choose to do so.	Varies

Childcare settings that are registered to run early years care and education for children will need to follow the Early Years Foundation Stage (EYFS) Framework. This is a set of standards which must be followed to make sure that children 'learn and develop well and are kept healthy and safe' (EYFS Statutory Framework 2014). If settings are registered and inspected by Ofsted, they will need to show how they are meeting the quality and standards of provision. To find out more about the EYFS, see page 20.

Some early years workers may prefer to care for children in their own homes as registered childminders

Extend

Looking at the table on page 3, explore the advantages and disadvantages of each type of childcare setting.

1.2 Identify some of these settings within local provision (D2 A1)

Are you able to explain what local childcare provision means? It means what kind of childcare is available in your local area. There is likely to be a range of different childcare providers from large to small, and these will be funded and run in different ways. This section is about what is available, how they are funded and the differences between different types of childcare provision.

Childcare settings also help parents of young children who work. There are some free entitlements for early education and childcare for all three- and four-year-olds, and also for some two-year-olds, which parents have to register and apply for depending on what best suits them and their child. Parents will have to meet specific criteria in order to be eligible for free childcare.

Find out more about …

… the entitlements to free childcare for children in England which is issued by the Department for Education (DfE)

Activity

Choose a childcare setting in your local area and look at the information which is available on their website. How is the information organised?

Extend

What does the website tell you about the setting and how it is run?

Activity

Looking at the table on page 3 in the previous section, add a column on the right ('Type of provision') and fill in the type of provision which the setting would be, for example voluntary, private, statutory or independent. Remember that some settings may be more than one – for example a school-based nursery could be independent or maintained.

Types of setting

- **Voluntary** – this means provision which has been set up and funded by donations and voluntary contributions. It may, for example, be run by a charity or church group in the local community, and parents may have to pay a donation to help cover costs. In some cases parents or carers may stay and supervise their children so that they can socialise with others, but the ways in which these operate vary. If children are left with staff, the setting will need to be registered with and inspected by Ofsted.
- **Private** – this means that parents need to pay for the provision as it is run privately. This may include settings such as a crèche, a workplace nursery, private day nursery or a childminder's home. These settings will need to be registered with and inspected by Ofsted if they are providing regular care and education for children. For example, a childminder will need to be registered and inspected, but a crèche which may just provide care from time to time does not.
- **Statutory/maintained** – this term is used for settings which are government-funded as they have to be available by law, such as schools. They will be registered and inspected by Ofsted. They may also be known as 'maintained' settings.
- **Independent** – this term is usually used for independent schools which are not paid for by government or state funding, so parents will be charged for them. Independent schools will still have to follow the EYFS Framework and are also inspected by Ofsted.

Top marks

In order to meet the assessment criteria for the assignment for this unit, you will need to show that you understand the differences between types of provision which are available for children aged 0–5 years.

Give examples of three different types of childcare settings and outline their main features.

Create a leaflet for parents which describes the different types of early years settings and where these might be found in your local area.

Read and write

Both the 'Find out more about …' and the 'Top marks' tasks ask you to write down what you can about different settings in your local area. You will need to research and read about this by looking locally, through using your local library or children's centre, for what is available in your area. You might also look online at your local Children's Information Service or local authority website.

Five things to know about childcare settings

1) Registered early years settings need to follow the EYFS Framework and are inspected by Ofsted.
2) There are three main types of early years provision: statutory, voluntary and private.
3) Childminders and nannies provide the most flexible provision.
4) Schools and school-based nurseries will only run during the term.
5) Working parents have some free childcare entitlements.

Grading

In order to achieve assessment criteria 1.1 and 1.2 and also to achieve grading criteria D2 and A1, you will need to:

Identify settings within local provision from across the sectors.

Discuss the differences between types of provision available for children aged from birth to five years.

■ Learning Outcome 2: Understand how to prepare for placement

Although you will not need a placement for this qualification, if you plan to work with children you will need to spend some time in one as part of your ongoing training and development. Many higher level childcare qualifications are work-based, which means that you will need to have a placement in an early years setting so that you can show that you have the skills to put your knowledge into action. This section is about the kinds of things you need to know about and how to make sure that you are well prepared. The more preparation you put in to finding a good placement and making sure that you are ready, the more likely it is to be a positive experience.

High priority

Remember what a placement is for: it is about checking that you are ready for work – both in what you know and in the way in which you behave towards children and adults.

Assessment criteria grid

Learning outcomes	Assessment criteria
The learner will:	The learner can:
2. Understand how to prepare for placement.	2.1. Describe key issues to consider when preparing for a placement with children, including dress code, behaviour, time keeping and positive attitudes.

2.1 Describe key issues to consider when preparing for a placement with children (D3 B1)

Work placements are valuable because you can find out what this kind of work is really about on a day-to-day basis. They are useful both to you and to the people you are working for, because they have an additional team member and you can see whether the early years environment is as you expected. Even if you do not end up working in a childcare setting, many of the placement guidelines here will carry over to other places of work. You will need to think about what is important and remind yourself about this, both before you start and during your placement.

Also remember that in the future you may need to ask for references from early years settings where you have been on placement, so it is always a good idea to do as good a job as you can.

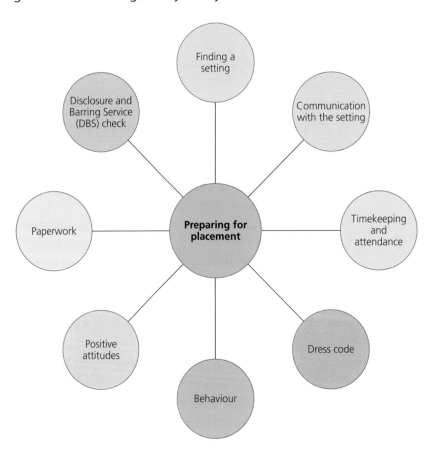

Finding a setting

You may be asked to find your own placement or your tutor may do this for you. If you have this responsibility, you should have some support and guidance from your school or college so that you can find the best placement for you. In either case, you will need to think about the following:

- What kind of setting is it? Would you like to work with a childminder or in a larger setting, perhaps a nursery or a school? Think about what might be involved with each and where you would like to gain experience. If you have seen what is involved in one type of setting, you should try another so that you can widen your experience: it may not be as you expect.

- Can I get there easily? Check that you can reach the setting by public transport and be there on time, or if you are able to drive, whether you will be able to park.
- What is the age range of the children? Think about the age range and remember that it is a good idea to have experience with different ages as this will help you to decide the age you would like to work with later on.
- Do they have placements available for the time I need it? Even if they do offer placements, you may find that the setting has several students already and are unable to offer you the dates you need. Try to plan for a first, second and possibly even a third choice for your placement.

Remember that you can find out about settings by looking at their websites as well as Ofsted reports. It is a good idea to be in a setting which demonstrates good or outstanding practice so that you can have the best possible experience throughout your placement.

Communication with the setting

You will need to phone, visit or email different settings to enquire whether they take students on placement, or you may need to communicate with one to confirm the placement which has been set up by your school or college. There will be advantages to each of these ways of communicating and you can choose the one you are happiest with. Remember that it is very important that you do this yourself – the work placement is for you. Do not ask your parents or anyone else to do it for you.

- Phone – make sure you introduce yourself and explain why you are calling. Ask to speak to the person responsible for student placements and make sure you have all the information you need, for example the dates or times you need to go, as well as the age of the children. If you are phoning, be prepared to call back as it may not be a convenient time for the placement co-ordinator. Remember to be polite and to thank those you speak to for their help.
- Setting visit – if you pass a setting regularly, you may decide to visit in person. If you do this, it is unlikely that you will be able to speak to the placement co-ordinator in person without an appointment but the office may be able to advise you whether placements are available or make an appointment for you.
- Email – before you write your email, think about the information you need to include, including any particular areas or ages of the children you are interested in working with, or what you need to confirm. In your email you should introduce yourself and state the timescale of your placement as well as giving information about your school or college and course. You must always remember to thank the person you are addressing it to.

Write a letter or email to a setting asking whether a placement is available. Address it to the placement or placement co-ordinator. Remember to include all the points above as well as your own contact details and when you would need to start your placement.

What are the advantages of visiting the settings in person?

Jargon buster

Placement co-ordinator – person responsible for managing students that are on placement in the setting.

Once you have found your setting and arranged a start date, it is a good idea to arrange a pre-placement visit with the setting so that you can go through details such as:

- where you will be and who you will be working with, so that you are familiar with where you need to go and who you will meet
- any tasks which you need to complete whilst on your placement, and any paperwork which you should show the placement co-ordinator before you start
- where you should go for your break and the location of toilets
- a note of names and rooms so that you are ready on your first day.

If your route to the setting is unfamiliar to you, it will also be helpful to make the journey to find out exactly where it is and how long it will take you to get there.

Timekeeping and attendance

Make sure you know the name of your key contact before you start at the setting so that you can ask for them when you arrive on your first day. A work placement is like a job and you should think of it in the same way: good timekeeping and attendance are essential. You will need to be on time for each session, and ideally early to make sure you know what you should be doing, but you should not arrive late. This sends the message that you do not view your placement or your work there as important.

In the same way, if you are supposed to be attending on a particular day, you must make sure you always do unless you are ill or have a good reason. If you cannot be there, always phone your placement co-ordinator as soon as you can to say that you will not be able to attend. Others will be relying on you and will have planned for you to be there to carry out a particular activity or supervise a group of children. It can be very frustrating to be let down, particularly if they need a set number of adults, and this also sends the message that you are unreliable.

Five things to know when preparing for placement

1) Carefully research the settings which are available for your placement.
2) Make sure you always communicate clearly and politely with your placement co-ordinator.
3) Know the name of the person you are going to meet and make sure you have contacted and visited them before you start your placement.
4) Always arrive on time or a little early if possible on placement days.
5) Inform the placement as soon as you can if you are unable to go in.

Dress code

This is about what you wear to a placement and your general appearance at work. You should remember that even on work experience, you are acting as a member of staff. You will need to behave in a professional way, and this includes what you wear. The way you dress and appear to others will send messages to those around you, including the children. For example, if you go for your first visit looking untidy or wearing inappropriate clothing, this does not give a professional message. When you first go to visit your placement you should ask them about their dress code and be aware of what staff are expected to wear. If you are not sure, always ask before you start – this will be seen as positive as it shows you have thought about it and want to do the right thing.

Why is it important to dress appropriately for work placements?

Aspects of a dress code

Clothing	Ideally, what you wear in an early years setting should be practical but smart. It should also be comfortable and easy to wash as you are likely to be working with children on messy activities such as painting. Check whether you can wear jeans or shorts. T-shirts with slogans or messages should also be avoided if possible. If you are female, remember you will be crouching or leaning down to young children's level for much of the time, so low cut tops or short skirts are not a good idea.
Religious dress	If you dress in a particular way as part of your religion, this should not be a problem with the setting as it is discriminatory to ban articles of clothing on religious grounds.
Jewellery and make up	Remember that you are working in a practical environment and that you should not need to wear very much make up or jewellery. Long or hooped earrings, or necklaces which are on view, are not a good idea if you are working with babies and toddlers as they will pull them and you may be hurt. For hygiene reasons, nails should be short, as you will be helping to prepare food and drinks for the children.
Footwear	Flat shoes are the most practical footwear when working with very young children as you do not want to risk tripping over and you may have to move quickly to help children or prevent an accident. However, there are also some exceptions to this; for example, it is unlikely that you would be able to wear flip flops during the summer for health and safety reasons. If you want to wear trainers, you should check with the setting as to whether they are part of the dress code.
Personal hygiene	When you first start working with young children, you will find that you are more prone to catching coughs and colds and other infections. You should make sure that you wash your hands regularly to reduce the chance of picking up any illnesses. Keep your nails clean and long hair tied back so that you are less likely to pass on or pick up germs. You also need to be aware that young children can easily pass on head lice, and this is not an indication of dirty hair; head lice is spread by direct contact.
Tattoos and piercings	Some employers may ask you to cover any visible tattoos and to remove piercings while at work. While the piercings may not be appropriate for practical reasons, more employers are allowing some tattoos. You should check their dress code or policy to clarify what is permitted.

Behaviour

In some cases your placement will give you an induction which is an introduction to what you are expected to do. They may also go through a handbook to give you some guidance as to what is expected of you while you are there. This will help you to think about key points, and you can re-read it if you need to remind yourself of anything.

While you are on your placement, you will be expected to behave in a particular way. This includes the way in which you talk to others and how you act in a work environment. You should not talk about other members of staff in a negative way, for example, gossiping. You are part of the team and all staff should be working together for the benefit of the children. You should also know that the setting will have policies about different things, for example, the use of mobile phones, and you will need to know what these are and follow them (for more information on this, see page xx).

You must also remember that you are a role model to the children and that they will want to copy what you do. For example, if you are sitting at the table with them during snack or lunch time, show them good table manners and encourage them to behave in the same way.

Jargon buster

Role model – someone who is looked up to by others as an example.

Theory in action

Simon is working in a pre-school on a work placement and has to be there for two sessions a week. He has to travel by bus to reach the placement and is usually five to ten minutes late. His placement co-ordinator has spoken to Simon today, and he is unhappy as she has told him that this is not acceptable while he is on placement. He needs to arrive on time so that his supervisor can talk to him about what she needs him to do. Simon has started to talk to the other staff about what has happened and is complaining to them about how he is being treated by the supervisor.

- What do you think about Simon's reaction?
- What should he do now?

Positive attitude

This may sound obvious but when speaking to others in your placement, you should show a positive attitude as much as you can. This is about the way in which you relate to others; for example, smiling and showing respect to others, being willing to help with the smaller things as well as what you are doing, and going the extra mile through doing extra things to help.

Ways in which you can demonstrate a positive attitude whilst on placement

Smiling and being positive with children and adults	Remember that if you are cheerful and greet others with a smile, you are more likely to develop positive relationships with them. You can also show that you enjoy working with children by talking to them as much as you can, getting down to their level so that you can see each other's reactions, and listening to what they are saying to you.
	With adults, it may just be about making small talk or greeting them at the start of the day. Everyone is busy and has their own problems but a pleasant hello can make all the difference. You should also remember to be polite – it will go a long way if you remember to thank people for their help.
Offering to help where possible	When you are being given instructions, always ask if you have any questions as you think of them so that you can do the best you can. If you finish what you have been asked to do, always see if you can do anything further to help.
Going the extra mile	Offer to do extra things for the setting when you can, such as helping with a Christmas fair or offering to go on a trip, even if it is not on your normal placement day if you can be available. This is all good experience as you are likely to be doing these kinds of things when you are employed, and it also shows that you are committed to your role.
Look out for extra things to do	Always look out for extra things you can do to help. For example, if you notice that there is something on the floor or a mess needs clearing up, offer to do it rather than stepping over it or thinking that it is not your responsibility. If a child is upset or needs extra help with something, talk to them while checking with your supervisor that they are happy with this. These kinds of actions will all help to show that you are keen to develop as an early years worker and will make you a pleasure to have around.

Why is it important to have a positive attitude when you are on your placement?

Paperwork

Your college will also be likely to provide an attendance register which the setting will need to sign each time you attend, and you will need to show that you have completed a set number of hours to pass your course. You should be organised with this because it is your responsibility to ensure that it is completed and not that of your tutor or work placement. Staff in early years settings will always be busy and you should not give them more to do if at all possible.

DBS check

When you reach the age of 16, you will also need to have a DBS check before you start at your setting. Your setting or college tutor will tell you what you need to do and where you should get the paperwork you need to complete, and you will not be able to work unsupervised with children until it has come through. Once you start your job with children, it will need to be renewed approximately once every three years.

Jargon buster

DBS – this stands for Disclosure and Barring Service which was previously known as CRB or Criminal Records Bureau check. This process will check against a central register to make sure that you do not have previous criminal convictions. It is an important part of the safeguarding process for keeping children safe. It is required for any job – either paid or unpaid – in which you work with children or young people under 18. To find out more about DBS, go to https://crbdirect.org.uk/.

My life as a placement co-ordinator

My name is Stella and I work in a large nursery in the centre of town. One of the roles I have in the setting is as placement co-ordinator for students who come to do their work experience with us as part of their early years course. I am available as their mentor and to make sure their placement runs smoothly.

We are close to a college and large secondary school so we are often asked to take students on placement. Some of the best students we have are those who are reliable and organised, and who act professionally from the beginning. This means that we have less to do as we do not need to speak to them about their behaviour or timekeeping and can keep our attention for the children, which is our main role. We also appreciate students who obviously enjoy working with the children and who ask questions if they are unsure about anything.

Jargon buster

Mentor – an experienced advisor who acts as a guide and support for those who need it.

Find out more about ...

… some of the different roles of staff you might come across in an early years setting. Are all of these job roles based in the setting, or are some of them based elsewhere?

Read and write

Make a list of some of these roles so that you can find out who is responsible for them when you go on your own placement.

Check what you know

Make a checklist using bullet points that you can use to help you when you are preparing to start a placement in an early years setting.

Extend

Think about other ways in which you could show employers that you are committed to your placement.

Five things to know when starting on a placement

1) Look smart and dress appropriately.
2) Behave in a professional way towards others.
3) Act as a good role model for the children.
4) Be positive and offer your help when you can.
5) Be organised and take any paperwork with you.

Grading

In order to achieve assessment criteria 2.1 and also to achieve grading criteria D3 and B1, you will need to:

Describe key issues to consider when preparing for a placement with children.

Explain the importance of meeting key issues in preparation for working with children aged from birth to five years.

■ Learning Outcome 3: Understand the responsibilities and limits of the early years worker in placements

High priority

Remember, never take action in a situation which you are not sure about. Speak to a more experienced member of staff.

Assessment criteria grid

Learning outcomes	Assessment criteria
The learner will:	The learner can:
3. Understand the responsibilities and limits of the early years worker in placements.	3.1. Identify responsibilities of early years workers, recognising when they should refer to others.

What do your responsibilities mean? As a student, your main responsibilities are to make sure that you attend your classes and complete your coursework on time. However, when you are on a work placement your role is as a member of staff and you need to be aware of an additional set of responsibilities, particularly because you are working with children. Your tutor and placement supervisor will advise you, and you must learn to act in a professional way towards others. However, although you should have been told about what you need to do when on a placement, sometimes you may find that you are confronted with situations which you do not expect or know how to deal with. This section is about the responsibilities and limits of your role and what you should do if you have any concerns or need to pass on information.

3.1 Identify responsibilities of early years workers, recognising when they should refer to others (D4 B2)

Your responsibilities are the things which are expected of you as an early years worker on placement. You should remember that in a placement situation, you need to take an active part as well as watching what is happening. Members of staff have a job description which sets out what they have to do as part of their role, and your setting may have a similar list of responsibilities for those who are on work placements. The kinds of responsibilities you have are likely to be similar to those in the job description of an early years assistant, although you may not be required to attend meetings or contribute towards planning. You will need to show that you are responsible through your awareness of these issues and acting on them when necessary, so that you can show that you are work-ready. Your learner handbook will also guide you by identifying a range of competencies that you must achieve in placement.

Responsibilities of an early years worker on placement

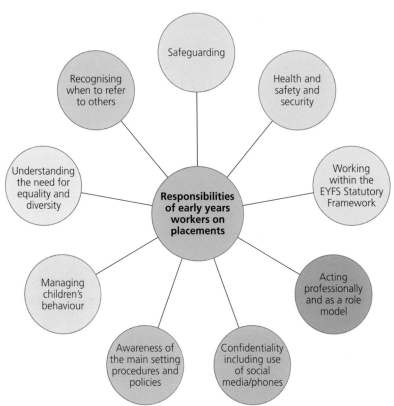

Safeguarding

You may have heard the word 'safeguarding' when talking about work with children. Safeguarding is the responsibility of all those who work in early years settings, and it is about how we protect children in their everyday surroundings. This concerns issues such as general health and safety as well as 'stranger danger' and what happens outside the early years environment. Your setting will have a safeguarding policy which you should read if you are on a placement there as a member of staff.

If you suspect anything or notice something which concerns you, you should speak to another member of staff or ideally to the setting's child protection officer as soon as you can. It may be that others have not seen it, and your responsibility is always to think about the child's safety. Remember: the consequences of doing nothing may be long-lasting and are potentially dangerous for the child.

You should not be completely on your own with children, in particular if you are under 17 as this is a requirement of the EYFS statutory guidance. If you are over 17, you should have received your DBS certificate, as settings will be aware of the need for safeguarding. You should also take care with how much physical contact you give young children, as they will often want to hug adults or sit on their knee. Watch other adults around you and note how much contact they use, as this will be the most appropriate for the age and stage of the children you are working with.

Theory in action

Gemma has recently started on a work placement in a large pre-school and enjoys working with young children. During story time, the children want to sit near her and on her lap. This has started to cause a problem as every day there is an argument between the children about whose turn it is. The pre-school manager has told her that as it has become disruptive each time, she should tell them to sit next to her instead.

- Give two reasons why it is important for Gemma to carry out the manager's wishes.
- What should she do if she finds it difficult and the children do not listen to her?

Health, safety and security

This is a wide area and you will need to be familiar with its main aspects. As well as knowing about safeguarding, you should be familiar with other health and safety issues.

- **Keeping children safe and secure** – all early years settings now have keypads or locked entrances so that they are secure, and staff are aware of who is coming in and out of the building. There will also be signing-in books and name badges so that everyone knows who is on the site in case the building needs to be evacuated, for example, in a fire. If you see people you do not recognise, or who do not have a badge, you should always speak to another member of staff to check that they have been signed in for security purposes.

- **Fire drills** – your setting should have regular fire drills so that children and staff know what to do in an emergency. If you have not been present for a fire drill, make sure you know what your responsibilities are and where you need to leave the building, as well as the position of the assembly point outside.

- **First aid and dealing with accidents and injuries** – your setting will be required to have one or more members of staff who are paediatric first aiders so that at least one will be available at any one time. A list of first aiders will usually be displayed in the setting office or next to first aid boxes. You should not give first aid unless you are a trained first aider, so you should know the names of the setting's first aiders so that you can find them quickly if needed. In this situation, you may need to comfort children and calm them down while they are waiting for help to arrive.

Why is it important that all staff are aware who is entering and leaving the setting?

- **Managing sickness and storage of medicines** – your setting will need to keep medicines in a locked cabinet for those children who need to keep them on site, for example, those who are asthmatic or who need an Epipen in case of allergic reactions. Medicines should only be given to children by a first aider and with the permission of parents, and this should always be recorded with the dose, date, time and signature. If you notice that a child is unwell, you should make sure you pass this information on as soon as possible.

Theory in action

You are in the setting's office on your own for a few moments while the office receptionist is speaking to someone. A parent comes to the door with some medicine and tells you that it is for her child. She gives you the child's name but says that she is in a hurry and cannot fill in or sign the form which is required by the setting before administering the medicine. You are unsure what to do but take the medicine for her and she leaves. You are tempted just to leave the medicine on the desk for the office receptionist to find when she comes back.

- What should you do now?
- Why is it important that you speak to someone about what has happened?

- **Storage of equipment** – everyone working with children should know that untidy or incorrect storage can be a safety hazard. This is because if items are not put away correctly, they can cause harm. For example, if you store boxes on top of cupboards which overhang, they can fall on top of people when they open the cupboard doors. Make sure that you do not put away any broken or damaged equipment: tell another member of staff so that it can be repaired or thrown away and does not hurt anyone. This is part of a risk assessment. Be careful when you are getting out and putting away equipment, particularly if it is heavy or high up. You should not take risks or put yourself in danger. If you are concerned, ask someone else to help you or speak to your supervisor.

- **Storage of hazardous materials** – be careful where you put cleaning materials or anything which may be hazardous. They should be kept high up or in a locked cupboard so that they cannot be reached by young children.
- **Preparing resources and materials** – this should not involve anything which is unsafe, but always look at what you have set up afterwards just to make sure. For example, check that floors are not wet if you are setting up a messy activity, to ensure that no one falls over. If you are going to use any electrical equipment for the activity, only use what has been supplied by the setting as it will need to have been tested.
- **General health and safety** – you should be aware of general health and safety issues such as things left lying on the floor which could be a trip hazard, or chairs sticking out rather than pushed under tables, and encourage the children to do the same. Your setting will have a health and safety policy which you should read so that you are clear about what to do in health and safety situations. If you keep health and safety in mind as part of your day-to-day practice, it will soon become second nature to you and you will also be acting as a good role model to the children.

Five things to know about health and safety

1) Remember that all adults in the setting have a responsibility to keep children safe and secure.
2) Make sure you know where fire exits are and how to get out of the building quickly.
3) Remember to think about health and safety issues when getting equipment and resources out and putting them away.
4) Know the names of first aiders in the setting.
5) Look out for hazards in the learning environment and act on them as soon as you can.

Working with the EYFS – The Early Years Foundation Stage

If you are working with young children you should have looked at the EYFS Statutory Framework. You can find it online at www.gov.uk. It is the set of guidelines which are used by all those who work with young children and is statutory for early years settings. The EYFS is made up of three sections: the learning and development requirements, assessment, and safeguarding and welfare requirements including First Aid.

1   **The Learning and development requirements** – these are about what the children need to know and do as they grow and learn. The learning and development requirements are divided into seven different areas:

Prime areas:
- **Communication and language** – this is about speaking, listening and understanding and giving children opportunities to practise and develop their skills in expressing themselves.
- **Physical development** – this is about giving children the opportunity to develop their physical skills and co-ordination through a range of activities, as well as learning about the importance of physical activity and healthy eating.
- **Personal, social and emotional development** – this means the development of a positive sense of self, starting to learn social skills and forming relationships with others, as well as learning to manage their feelings and behaviour.

Specific areas:
- **Literacy** – this is about encouraging children to begin to link sounds and letters so that they can start to read and write.
- **Mathematics** – this is a wide area and includes the development of children's skills in counting and using numbers as well as being able to describe simple shapes and starting to use measures.
- **Understanding the world** – this is giving children the opportunity to find out about their world and local community. They should have the chance to talk about and discuss their local environment as well as finding out more about different people.
- **Expressive arts and design** – this area is about giving children the opportunity to explore a range of media and materials, and also having the chance to express themselves through the areas of art, role play, music and movement.

2   **Assessment** – this is about how adults assess children's learning and development, or look at how well they are making progress. Assessment is done in different ways, but it is mainly through observing children over time to look at their interests and the way in which they learn as individuals. This will be the responsibility of staff at the setting but you may be asked to observe and note down how individual children respond in different situations. However, if you are asked to observe children, make sure you understand exactly what you need to do and how to record it (for more information on this, see page 88).

3   **The Safeguarding and welfare requirements** – this is about staffing and adult/child ratios, making sure the environment is safe and secure, safeguarding and health and safety (for more information on this, see page 17).

Find out more about …

… the EYFS. Choose one of the three sections and report back to others in your group about what you have found out.

Five things to know about the EYFS

1) The EYFS is statutory for all registered early years settings.
2) It sets the standard for learning, development and care for children from birth to five years.
3) There are seven areas of learning and development.
4) Practitioners need to assess children in an ongoing way so that they can plan activities effectively for children based on interest and need.
5) All adults must take steps to ensure that children are kept safe and well.

Acting professionally and as a role model

As we have already discussed, it is important to remember that you are acting as a professional, even when working on placement. You will need to make sure that your behaviour and the way in which you act towards others shows this: it means that you will need to think about your actions and behaviour at all times. Look at the way other adults in the setting behave, particularly with the children: remember that you are there to support their learning and development, guide them and act as a role model. Children will look up to you as an adult and someone who they can trust, and you should make sure that you act accordingly. Also remember that *not* acting in some situations can be dangerous to others.

Activity

Consider the situations listed below and discuss in groups how the student is acting unprofessionally. What might happen if they do not act or do the wrong thing in each situation?

- not mixing with other staff in the setting during breaks but going outside to use a mobile phone
- slipping on a wet patch on the floor but not telling anyone else about it or clearing it up
- forgetting to sign in and out of the setting
- talking about the parents and children in the setting to friends when socialising
- asking the children to lock the gate when coming in rather than doing it themselves.

Theory in action

Sam has just started on a placement in a pre-school. She has been asked to tidy up in the messy area while a member of staff reads to the children on the carpet. While this is taking place, Sam starts talking to another adult in the room and this begins to distract the children. She is also being quite noisy with her tidying up. The member of staff who is reading the story is visibly unhappy and keeps looking over to Sam but she does not notice.

- Why is Sam not acting professionally? What example is she setting to the children?
- How might this impact on the children?
- What kind of impression is Sam setting?

Confidentiality including use of social media/phones

A topical issue when thinking about acting in a professional way is the use of social media. When on placement you must be very careful what you post, as this should not relate to the setting, the staff or children or your work there. Remember that what you write can be seen by others for a long time to come, and that posting without thinking can cause upset and harm to others.

Confidentiality is about the way you treat information which you are given as part of your role. In an early years setting you may find that you are told about children's backgrounds or things which are happening to them because you need to know – for example, if a child's parents are separating and this is affecting their child's behaviour. You should not pass this information to others outside the setting or talk about them, as this information is confidential. This may be particularly difficult in a small local setting, or if you are friendly with parents of children socially. However, confidentiality needs to be taken seriously. If you are unsure whether you should pass on information to others outside the setting, the best advice is not to.

Theory in action

Sandy is on a work placement in a small nursery in a village setting. She goes out each day to get her lunch from the bakers over the road. She has just heard that one of the parents has been diagnosed with a terminal illness, as the child's key person has told her. Sandy has been upset by the news and knows the lady working in the bakery who can see she is upset, so she tells her.

- What might be the consequences of this action?
- What can Sandy do now?

Use of mobile phones will not be allowed inside the setting, and you must not take any photographs of children with your own phone at any time; the setting is likely to include this in their confidentiality or safeguarding policy. There will be cameras or other equipment for photographing children which belong to the setting, and these cannot be removed: you may use them to gather evidence of children's learning and development while you are on site or on setting trips so that all photographs of children are kept in one place. Always ask for permission to use any equipment.

Awareness of the main setting', procedures and policies

Finding out about these should be part of your induction, but you should know the setting's requirements concerning a range of issues. These may include who to go to for first aid and what to do if there is an accident, health and safety issues and concerns, and the importance of confidentiality. The policies will include procedures to show how the setting requires you to act. Your mentor or supervisor should be able to show you where policies are kept as they will be available for staff and parents to read when needed; alternatively, they may be available to read on the setting's website.

> ### Read and write
>
> Find a list of policies for an early years setting which is local to you. Make a list of the main policies which you need to know about and under each one, note down the key information using bullet points.

Managing children's behaviour

As an adult working in the role of an early years worker, you will need to learn to manage the behaviour of children while you are on placement. This may be if they are working with you, or in your care while carrying out an activity. You may notice children behaving in a way which is not appropriate while sitting on the carpet, moving around inside the setting or in the outside area.

There are a number of important points you need to know when you are managing children's behaviour:

1 Make sure you know as much as possible about effective behaviour management when you start your placement. The setting will have a behaviour policy which you should read through so that you know what to do. There will be different strategies and sanctions with children.

2 Remember that you are on work placement as a professional. Be careful not to befriend the children too much or play with them as you might do with a younger brother or sister. This will make it more difficult if you have to speak to them about their behaviour.

3 Be careful of the language you use when managing behaviour. Try to tell children that the behaviour is wrong – for example, 'that was an unkind thing to do' – rather than telling them that *they* are unkind, as this will reinforce their own image of what they are good at.

4 Make it clear to children that they have a choice about their behaviour and that the responsibility for the correct choice is theirs. If they choose to behave negatively then they should know what will happen.

5 Praise children for doing the right thing and make sure that you notice good behaviour as well as incorrect choices.

6 Be confident when you are managing behaviour and use a voice which makes it clear to children when they are or are not making the correct choices. You should also be careful what you say to children as you should always follow up on any action. Young children will be able to tell if you are not sure about what to do.

7 Remember that children will copy adults – be a good role model and always stay calm when managing behaviour.

Jargon buster

Strategies – ways in which adults can encourage positive behaviour. For example, through verbal praise, stickers or other methods of encouragement.

Sanctions – These are the ways in which adults manage behaviour, often using a scale. For example, some settings may use the sanction of a smiley face chart for children's names which goes to a sad face and then a frown for inappropriate behaviour. The children might then know that the next step is 'time out'.

Activity

Rhodri is enjoying his placement and particularly supporting children's physical development in the outside area. He is very sporty himself and has been working with the children on their throwing and catching, jumping and running skills. However, he likes to play with them as well. Today the children have become over-excited and are not doing what he is asking them.

● What can Rhodri do now?
● How could he have managed the situation more effectively?

Theory in action

Soriya, aged three, is playing in the sand with two other children, and you are close by. One of them takes Soriya's spade away while she is using it and she starts to throw sand in their faces.

● Describe step by step how you would manage the children's behaviour in this situation.

Extend

- Why is it important that behaviour strategies are very clear to children?
- How can early years workers ensure that this is the case?

When you are on placement, make sure you watch how experienced adults manage behaviour. They will use lots of different strategies, and might vary these with different children according to their needs. Managing behaviour is something that you will need to learn, but if you have any concerns about how to do this while you are on placement, you should always refer to a more experienced member of staff.

When you are on placement you will need to look at how experienced staff work with groups of children

Equality and diversity

You should have an understanding of these terms and know what they mean. Equality and diversity are words which are used when we talk about ensuring that all children are treated equally, no matter what their race, gender or abilities. When you are working with children, it is one of your responsibilities to ensure that you support inclusion through the way you value all children and respect their human rights. For more information on equality and diversity, see pages 34 and 43.

Jargon buster

Equality – being equal, especially in terms of rights and opportunities.

Diversity – understanding that each person is unique while recognising individual differences.

Inclusion/Inclusive Practice – making sure that all children are included in the setting through giving equal access and opportunity and removing discrimination.

You may be asked to set up different areas in the learning environment

Recognising when to refer to others

Knowing when you should refer to others is also one of your responsibilities. Much of what you are doing on placement is building up your experience, and looking at how others in the setting manage different situations. However, when starting to work in a new placement, you will be taking on a lot of new information. As well as learning how to behave in a work environment and act professionally, you will be finding out all about the setting and how it is run, looking at important legislation and policies, working with the children and their parents, and learning to work with other staff. This is a lot to learn all at once and you will probably feel that it is difficult to remember everything. You should ask any questions as they come up if you can, or make a note of them, as you may forget during the course of the day. You will need to be clear on who you can ask and when you can ask – although obviously you will need to ask immediately in some cases or if there is any danger to others.

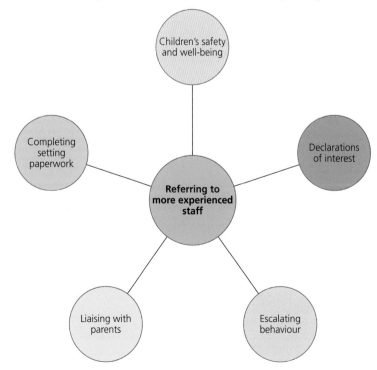

Children's safety and well-being

Children's safety is the most important area. If you have any concerns at all about a child's safety you should immediately report this to your supervisor or to the member of staff who is in charge of child protection or safeguarding. You should also be responsible yourself, both in the way you behave towards children and in making sure you do not do or bring anything to the setting which may harm them.

Declarations of interest

This may come up if you find that you know a child or the family of a child who is at the setting. This means that it may be difficult for you to have a personal as well as a professional relationship with the child and family. It is important that you pass on this information to staff because you could potentially find that you are put in a difficult situation. For example, the child's parents may call you by your first name when all adults at the setting are known as 'Mr', 'Mrs' or 'Miss'. In this situation you should always seek advice about whether anything needs to be done.

Theory in action

Bhumika has just started her placement at a nursery setting and has realised that she knows one of the children in the toddler room who is the daughter of a friend of her mum's. Bhumika does not say anything as she does not see it as a problem. However, a few weeks later the girl's mother asks Bhumika how her daughter is doing at nursery and starts asking her questions about different members of staff.

- What should Bhumika do?
- Could this situation have been avoided?

Escalating behaviour

If you are in a situation where you have tried to manage children's behaviour but this is not working, you should always refer to more experienced staff as soon as possible. This is because you might put children's safety at risk as well as that of others. Remember that you can always send an older child who is sensible to ask for help if no adults are close enough to attract attention.

Five things to know about your responsibilities

1) Make sure you read key policies when you start your placement.
2) Watch experienced practitioners to see how they react to children, particularly when managing behaviour.
3) Remember the importance of confidentiality.
4) Do not use your mobile phone inside the setting.
5) Act as a role model to children in all you do.

Liaising with parents

One of the key aspects of an early years worker is liaising with parents and carers. Although on placement you might not have the opportunity or time to develop your own relationships with them and this is not your responsibility, you can shadow a member of staff and get to know their key children and parents. However, ultimately they will be responsible for both receiving and passing on information between parents and the setting, and ensuring that it is given to other members of staff if necessary. If you are asked to pass on any messages about children, it is very important that you do this straight away. Similarly, if a parent starts talking to you about something which you feel is confidential or sensitive, you should stop them and tell them that they should speak to their child's key person.

My life as an early years worker

My name is Rob and I am an early years worker in a small nursery; I have been here for around three years. As part of my job role I am key person for 17 children. This means that I have to make sure my key children are settled and happy, and work alongside their parents to look at their development and learning. Each morning, I greet my key children and speak to their parents so that I know about any issues as they occur; in the same way I let parents know when they collect their child about anything which has happened that they need to know about. Parents also help me by letting me know about their children's achievements at home. For example, one of our 13-month-olds took his first steps yesterday; I have been able to record this in his development folder as well as putting it on our 'Wow wall', where we display children's achievements at home.

How does a key worker find out about the achievements of their children?

Completing setting paperwork

When on placement, you should not complete setting paperwork or records unless you have been asked to do so and shown how to do it. This is because settings will have their own way of completing and filing paperwork so that it is done correctly and key members of staff see it.

What might happen if you do not meet your responsibilities

When you are on placement, you must remember that your responsibilities as a student are significant and that each one is important. You must always think of the children and put their needs first in any situation. The consequences of not meeting them may mean that a child is put at risk or in danger, or that they are not getting the best opportunity to meet their own potential. Always remember that your responsibilities are towards the needs of the children, and put their well-being and development first.

Extend

How can settings ensure that these kinds of incidents do not happen?

Theory in action

Jakob, who is 18, is on a pre-school placement and goes on a walking visit to the local pet shop with a group of children as part of a larger group. There are a number of helpers on the trip and on the walk back, the children stop at the park for a snack and a drink. They sit at tables in the picnic area. Jakob asks one of the other helpers, Mia, to watch his group so that he can go for a cigarette. She agrees, but this means that Mia is watching too many children for the agreed adult/child ratios. One of the children starts coughing on his fruit and Mia goes to help him, which means that she is not able to keep an eye on both groups.

- What might happen if Mia is unable to watch all of the children?
- Who is at fault here – Mia or Jakob?

Additional things to find out on your placement

As well as your key responsibilities and knowing when to refer to others, there are some additional things which will be helpful for you to find out while you are working on placement so that you, the children and the setting can benefit as much as possible:

- being aware of key staff and their names and responsibilities
- knowing about the setting's everyday routines
- helping with record keeping
- preparing learning materials and resources
- working alongside a member of staff
- making time to meet your mentor.

Being aware of key staff and their names and responsibilities

As well as knowing your own responsibilities, you should have some idea about those of other members of staff. If you are in a large setting, it can be difficult to learn lots of names, particularly if you are learning first names as well as 'Mrs X' or 'Mr Y'. Set yourself the target of learning key ones first. There may be photographs on the wall to help you in the entrance area of the setting, or you might be given an organisational chart or staff list which can help you. The key names you should learn should be:

- **The nursery or setting manager** – this person will have responsibility for all the staffing, children and Ofsted requirements of the setting.
- **Your own mentor or the person you are shadowing** – this person will look after you while you are on placement and make sure that you are meeting the requirements of the setting as well as your course. They may have a range of different roles within the setting.
- **The child protection officer or safeguarding officer** – the Child Protection Officer will be responsible for making sure that the policy is kept up to date and that all staff are trained and aware of safeguarding issues. They will also be the person who staff go to if they have any concerns about a child, so you should speak to this person if you have any concerns about a child's welfare
- **The Special Educational Needs Co-ordinator (SENCO)** – it will be helpful for you to know who the SENCO is in your setting. This person is responsible for making sure that the needs of children who have special educational needs are being met (for more information on this, see page 41).
- **The health and safety representative and first aiders** – these are important as you will need to know who to go to with any health and safety issues or if you have a first aid emergency (for more on health and safety, see page 18).

These roles may vary between settings – for example, the setting manager may also be the safeguarding officer, and the SENCO may work in several early years settings – but you should still get to know who these key people are so that you can go to them quickly if and when you need to.

Knowing about the setting's everyday routines

You may remember having daily routines as a child, such as having a bath and a story at bedtime. Routines help children to develop their confidence and feel secure because they know what will happen next.

All settings have their own everyday routines. For example, they may stop activities for a drink and a snack at 10.15, have a story at 11.30 and have lunch at 12.00. These kinds of routines are important, and also help us when managing behaviour and co-operation as they are 'what we do at this time of day'. Young children will gradually start to become independent through being able to carry out their own routines without being reminded to do so.

Helping with record keeping

When you first go to your setting, your supervisor or mentor may ask you to help with record keeping so that you get to know the way in which this is done. Each child will have a folder, or learning journey, and this may be paper based or stored digitally: this is where information about the child's learning and development will be kept, including observations. You may for example be asked to file information in the children's folders or to observe children when they are playing. This is because all adults working with children are constantly looking at the way in which they are learning and developing, and need to collect evidence to back up what they are saying. If you are asked to observe children and write things down, you will need to have some training and support in what to look for and how this should be recorded, as settings record their observations in different ways. For more information about observations and why we carry them out. For more information about observations and why we carry them out, see page 35.

see page 35.

St Mary's Nursery Observation Sheet

Name of child... Date...............

Area of learning and development...

Commentary...

....

....

Preparing materials and resources

Depending on the hours you work in the setting, you will probably be asked to prepare materials and resources for the children on a regular basis. This may involve all kinds of tasks from setting up tables and different areas to helping others with displays or preparing different resources for particular activities. If you are asked to do this, you should have plenty of guidance as to what you will need to do.

Acting as a key person

The EYFS requires that each child in the setting has a key person who is one of the members of staff, and you may be working alongside one of them so that you can get more of an idea about what this involves. Each key person is responsible for a number of children and their role is to develop a close working relationship with parents and carers and support each child's individual needs. They will do this through careful monitoring of each child's learning and development as well as taking time to speak to parents or carers daily if possible. Each key person will then make other members of staff aware of any issues.

Making time to meet your mentor

You should have a mentor or someone at the setting who is there to talk things through with you. If possible, try to have a meeting at a set time each week so that you can discuss your placement, and also so that you can seek their advice if necessary. Your mentor is someone who will be able to offer you the benefit of their experience and help you with any paperwork to do with your placement. Make sure you always attend these meetings and that you rearrange them if they need to be cancelled.

How regularly should you meet your mentor?

My life on an early years placement

My name is Emma and I have just started my placement working in a Reception class in a school. I am enjoying it but have found that there is a lot to learn and that it is very different from my last placement in a small nursery, where I was working with babies. I feel that I have to ask the teacher and the teaching assistant about little things all the time, so now I have started to keep a notebook which means that I can ask all my questions at a time which is convenient, as they are always so busy! I have needed to refer to other staff quite a bit as the parents tend to ask me questions that I do not know the answers to. It's really helpful having a set time with my mentor each Thursday too so that I can check in and ask about how they think I am doing as well as ask questions.

Grading

In order to achieve assessment criteria 3.1 and also to achieve grading criteria D4 and B2, you will need to:

Identify responsibilities of an early years worker by recognising when they should refer to others.

Explain what may happen if the responsibilities of the early years worker are not met.

■ Learning Outcome 4: Understand individual needs and the necessity for fairness and inclusive practice

What are children's individual needs? You may hear this term used regularly when talking about children's early years care and development. Looking at children's individual needs and interests helps us to plan for their care and the way we support their progress. We also need to show that we follow inclusive practice, which means including all children regardless of culture and gender as well as disability or area of special need. In this section we will look at children's individual needs and how you can work in line with current diversity and inclusive practice.

High priority

You should make sure you know what the term 'inclusive practice' means. Inclusive practice is making sure all children are included in activities so that there are no barriers to their learning and development.

Assessment criteria grid

Learning outcomes	Assessment criteria
The learner will:	The learner can:
4. Understand individual needs and the necessity for fairness and inclusive practice.	4.1. Identify individual needs and ways of working that treat children fairly and in line with current diversity and inclusive practice.

4.1 Identify individual needs and ways of working that treat children fairly and in line with current diversity and inclusive practice (D5 A*)

Part of your role as an early years worker will be to treat all children fairly and meet their individual needs. The EYFS states that all those who work with children must plan for their needs through educational programmes which 'consider the individual needs, interests and stage of development of each child in their care'. This means that you should take time to get to know each child and their needs and interests, as well as looking at their age and stage of development, so that you can plan for them to have enjoyable experiences through each area of learning and development in the EYFS as well as keeping them happy and safe. It also means you must not favour some children more than others, or exclude any children from activities which others are doing: at all times you will need to treat children and their families with respect.

Identifying children's individual needs

All children have their own individual needs: every child is unique. Some will be confident and enjoy socialising with others, some may love dancing and music, others may know everything there is to know about trains or insects. They will also all learn and develop at different rates – some may walk, talk or learn to count earlier than others. However, we cannot respond to children's individual needs until we know what they are. We can identify children's individual needs by:

- using information forms
- observing children

- talking to children and finding out about their interests
- getting to know their families
- learning about any medical needs
- looking at their age and stage of development.

Using information forms

Before children start at the setting, their parents or carers will need to fill in a number of different information forms. These forms outline any important issues which the setting should be aware of, as well as the child's age and position in their family, their ethnicity, any health needs or allergies and so on. From this starting point the setting will start to build up a picture of the individual child.

Observing children

One way in which early years workers are able to identify children's individual needs is through observation: we need to watch them to see if they are happy and behaving normally, as well as being able to see how they are learning and developing.

How do observations help us to find out about children's needs and abilities?

When observing young children, the EYFS asks early years workers to focus mainly on the three prime areas of learning and development. The reason for this is that they are seen as the starting points for what children need to be able to develop and learn well overall. So when thinking about children's individual needs, we most often look at these three areas because they will have such an impact on how children think and behave, see unit 2, page 89.

The three prime areas of learning and development

Prime area of learning	Why it is important
Communication and language	Children are learning to communicate and use language so that they can think clearly, develop their own ideas, and start to express themselves.
Physical development	Children are learning to move around and control their bodies; they need to learn to keep healthy and safe as well as developing skills both in large and small movements.
Personal, social and emotional development	Personal, social and emotional development helps children to develop confidence and social skills. They will also learn to have respect for others and how to behave when in groups.

By looking carefully at different areas of a child's development, we can make sure that we build up a clear picture of each child's needs so that we know what will help them to be happy and safe. For example, a young child who has impaired vision will need their key person's support in learning to find their way around different areas of the setting when they first start; a child who has recently moved to the area may be more 'clingy' with their parents during 'drop off'.

For more information on observations and how we use them to measure children's development, see Unit 2 page 88.

Theory in action

Ryan is two years old and is very quiet. He has been attending Fairlands Nursery for several weeks. He does not like leaving his mother in the morning and takes some time to stop crying after she goes. He stays close to his key person for most of the time and needs lots of encouragement to become involved in what is happening.

Declan is the same age but is more confident. He is excited when he arrives at the setting and is starting to show a preference for the kinds of activities he likes. He is very curious and has no problem in trying out new things.
- What area of learning and development is being shown through the children's behaviour?
- What do you think you could do to support Ryan and develop his confidence? Think about the ways in which you could involve Ryan's parents at home as well as what the setting's involvement might be.

Extend

Could Declan's behaviour present any problems? If so, why?

Children's needs may also vary from time to time. Some, like those of Ryan and Declan, might be long term while others may be short term, such as being unsettled when they are going through a change such as moving house, or if they have a new brother or sister. This is one of the reasons why it is important to gather as much information as possible from children's families – it will give us a better picture of the whole child.

Talking to children and finding out about their interests

Early years workers should make the most of all opportunities to talk to children to help to meet their needs. This has many advantages – the more we talk to children, the more we help to develop their communication and language skills, the more we get to know them, and the more we find out about their interests. Children will enjoy telling you about the kinds of things which interest them and what they like to do. This will also help you to build up a relationship with them and make them more likely to tell you about things which are important to them.

Getting to know their families

Talking to children's families is another way in which we can measure their needs, and it is an important part of working with children. The key person should be the most important relationship which a child and their family have with the setting. The key person will liaise with the child's parents as well as other staff to make sure that the child's individual needs are being met in the setting and also to make other staff aware of what these are. There may be many things which families tell early years settings, from a child's sleep needs and routines to the fact that they are having problems with teething, or that they are excited about the birth of a new brother or sister. Getting to know families is always important and is particularly true when supporting children who have special educational needs and disabilities. For more on supporting special educational needs and disabilities (SEND), see page 40.

How does speaking to parents help us to meet children's needs?

Early years workers and particularly the key person will also need to be in close contact with parents so that they know about anything happening at home which might be affecting the child's mood or behaviour. Although parents will always be asked to let the setting know if there is anything wrong, or about any life events which might affect the child, they may not always remember to do this, especially if they are affected too.

The key person will also work closely with the SENCO if required and ensure that they are up to date with any paperwork, such as the education, health and care (EHC) plan (for more on this, see page 42).

Theory in action

Aabid is a very happy and lively four-year-old child who enjoys playing in the outdoor area of the setting and has many friends. However, his key person has noticed that for the last couple of days he seems withdrawn and is spending more time on his own. She asks his mother at pick-up time how he has been at home or whether she has noticed anything wrong. Aabid's mother says that his father and older brothers have gone back to Bangladesh to celebrate Eid with his family, and that this might be why.

- Could this be why Aabid is more withdrawn than usual?
- What kinds of things do you think you could do to support him?

Children who speak English as a second language are also likely to need some additional support in the setting, particularly in the earliest stages of learning to speak. This is because they will be tuning in to two, and sometimes more, different languages and trying to make sense of them. Parents should have outlined second language needs on forms before the child starts at the setting, but if the parents themselves do not speak good English this might not have happened. As you talk to parents and get to know their families, these kinds of needs may come to light. You will need to work with the child's key person as well as parents to support the child and work on strategies to help support their speech, language and communication development.

Find out more about ...

... supporting children who speak English as a second or additional language and meeting their needs. How can early years workers ensure that these children have the same opportunities as others?

Learning about any medical needs

Some children have medical needs or conditions which you will need to know about if you are working with them. These might mean that they need to be given medication at specific times of the day, or that medication needs to be kept in the setting in case they need it, for example, if they have asthma and need an inhaler. Some children might have food intolerances or allergies, and this should be clear so that all staff are aware of it to avoid any issues at snack times. In many settings, photos of children alongside their allergies are available in staff rooms or other staff areas so that there is no confusion. If staff do administer medication to children while in the setting, this will need to be recorded in a book.

Looking at their age and stage of development

Another thing to think about when looking at a child's needs is the child's age and stage of development. For example, we know that a child of one year will need to have at least one sleep per day and will also need to have their food mashed up or cut very small. Children's developmental needs will be accommodated in nurseries in different ways; for example, there is usually a 'baby room' because very small children will need more rest and quiet than those who are more mobile. There may also be a 'toddler room' for children who are under two and need more supervision. However, all children under five will need to have clear daily routines, and at least one secure attachment to an adult. For more on children's ages and stages of development, see Unit 2.

Age-related needs in the setting

Age of child	Age-related needs to consider in the setting (physical, communication and learning, social, emotional and behavioural)
0–1 year	Young babies need to be kept quieter in the setting than some of the older children. They need lots of physical contact and eye contact with adults. As they start to have more physical control, they need opportunities to develop muscles in their arms and legs, for example, through kicking. As they start to be able to pick things up, they will enjoy holding things which make a sound, or exploring different textures. They start to give adults more attention and to try to copy some actions and sounds.
1–2 years	Children start to become mobile and need to be kept safe in the setting as well as being provided with toys and equipment to support this; for example, small ride-on tricycles and push-along toys. Potty training may also be something that the setting can work on alongside parents. Children need plenty of opportunities to practise their language skills as these develop quickly at this age; use plenty of repetition such as patterns in stories and rhymes.
2–3 years	Children's emotional needs are strong at this age as they learn to assert themselves. They might have strong tantrums and become frustrated easily as they start to become more independent. Their physical needs are still developing, and they are able to use a spoon and crayon or pencil. Some may be dry through the night and able to use the toilet independently.
3–4 years	Children are very curious at this age and start to ask more questions. They need adults to continue to talk and listen to them to help to promote their communication and language skills. They are also able to sort simple objects and will start to count and repeat simple nursery rhymes. They are developing their control when holding a crayon or pencil and will be starting to throw and catch as well as kick a ball. They might also enjoy simple games such as lotto and snap. Children of this age are growing in independence and starting to develop friendships, as well as learning to share.
4–5 years	Children will be showing many signs of independence. They are still very attached to their primary carers but will also enjoy the company of other children. They should be able to dress themselves, although they might need some help with fastenings and are still developing other physical skills. They are starting to understand the needs of others and are be able to differentiate between right and wrong. They are able to reason and are starting to solve problems.

Children's ages will help us to think about what their needs might be. We can consider this particularly when thinking about developmental milestones such as walking, talking, potty training and so on. However, although we might use their age to help us, we need to remember that there will also be exceptions to this which we may or may not know about already; for example, if children have special educational needs or have suffered a trauma.

Theory in action

Millie is four years old and almost ready to start school. What might her needs be in terms of her age and stage of development? You can also use the stages of development in Unit 2 to help you.

Five things to know about identifying individual needs

1) Make sure you know about children's age and stage of development.
2) Be sure to get to know children so that you can tell if they are 'not themselves'.
3) Talk to children and their parents to find out about their needs and interests.
4) Speak to other staff if you are not sure about what is 'normal' for children's ages.
5) Talk to others about anything you notice, particularly if you have any concerns.

What are special educational needs?

When we talk about inclusion and inclusive practice, we often use this term to describe the inclusion of children who have special educational needs. This term includes a wide range of needs, medical conditions or disabilities which children may have. When children start to attend early years settings, these may already have been observed and acted upon by health professionals, but they may also be unknown as yet. This is another reason why it is so important for all adults to observe children and to discuss and note down anything which is a cause for concern.

Jargon buster

Special educational needs – children who have learning difficulties or a disability which makes it harder for them to learn than most children who are of the same age. This term is shortened to SEN, and is also sometimes referred to as special educational needs and disabilities (SEND).

Unit 1 An introduction to working with children aged 0–5 years

SENCO/Area SENCO – this means Special Educational Needs Co-ordinator. This person in your setting will make sure that the needs of children with SEN are being met, and will liaise with parents and professionals from outside the setting to support them.

When we talk about SEN, it can help to break them down into different areas. This can make it easier to tell them apart and to know how best to support children. SEN might be about children's social and emotional, communication and language, intellectual, physical or sensory needs.

- Social and emotional needs are to do with children's emotional development and their behaviour.
- Communication and language needs are about how children's language is developing and how they communicate with others.
- Intellectual or cognitive needs are about their ability to process information and apply it in different situations.
- Physical needs are about the development of children's physical skills. These may be about the growth, strength and development of their bodies and muscles in different parts of the body.
- Sensory needs are to do with children's senses: sight, hearing, touch, taste and smell. Most often in early years settings, sensory needs will relate to children's sight and/or hearing.

As an early years worker you will need to know about and support each child's individual needs.

All early years providers that are funded by the local authority must follow the statutory guidance for those who work with children who have SEND. While you will not need to be familiar with all aspects of legislation and Codes of Practice, you should know something about them. If children have severe needs or need support to access the curriculum, the setting may have funding so that they can have additional help from an adult. Parents and carers will also need support and there is always a guide published alongside a Code of Practice designed to help them.

Theory in action

Estelle and Jamie are twins, aged three-and-a-half years. They were born prematurely and their physical development has been affected: they are both considerably smaller and much less confident than other children when moving around the environment. Staff know this and both children have an education, health and care (EHC) plan so that their physical needs can be met, and to help everyone who has contact with them to know what these are. The plan says that they both need to do some exercises each day with their parents and their childminder to help them to develop more control in their muscles.

● Why is it important for all adults who are working with the children to know about their needs?

Jargon buster

Premature – this describes babies who are born earlier than expected, so are not fully developed in their mother's womb. Babies are normally considered 'full term' at 40 weeks. Twins and other multiple births may sometimes be born prematurely as there will be less space in the womb for them to develop.

Education, health and care (EHC) plan

This is a legal document which describes a child's special educational, health and social care needs. It also sets out the help that will be given to meet these needs.

Find out more about ...

... legislation and guidance including a Code of Practice, and find out what it says about SEN in the early years.

Extend

Break this information down into key points which early years workers will need to make sure they are aware of and report back to your group.

Treating children fairly and in line with current diversity and inclusive practice

It is important that all early years workers treat children fairly. This means that they will need to give everyone equal opportunities. Sometimes we discriminate against people without even knowing we are doing it; we might have negative ideas about what people can or cannot do before we meet them, based on what we know. It is important that we take time to get to know each child individually rather than base our thoughts on preconceived ideas.

You should remember that treating children equally does not necessarily mean treating them the same, but that you try to remove any barriers to them taking part; for example, if a child has a hearing impairment they might need to sit close to the adult. In all settings, all children should be given the opportunity to thrive and do well, whatever their circumstances.

Jargon buster

Equal opportunities – the right to be treated equally with others, and not discriminated against due to age, gender, race or disability.

Anti-bias practice – what the setting does to make sure that all children are treated fairly.

Discrimination – treating a person differently due to race, age, gender or disability.

Prejudice – assuming that you know something about a person before you know them, based on their race, age, gender or disability.

Theory in action

You are working with a group of children in the construction area. You notice that it is almost always the boys who choose to use these kinds of toys in your setting.

Ryan is three and has communication and language needs, which means he needs help to communicate with others. He is learning to use sign language but nobody in the nursery is trained to use it.

Melissa is four and is very good at puzzles. She wants to play with them all the time and needs a lot of encouragement from others to do something else.

Sophia is two and has just started at the nursery. She speaks no English and is learning Greek at home.

Billy finds it very hard to share and play with others. He is often on his own and he can be quite aggressive with other children when they approach him.
- What do you think about each of these situations?
- How could you as an early years worker try to include all children in what is happening?

There are two policies which all settings have which outline their guidelines when thinking about equal opportunities and special educational needs, although they may have slightly different names. These are the **SEND or Special Educational Needs policy** and the **Equality and diversity/ Inclusion and diversity policy.**

Find out more about ...

... these policies and what each of them means for you as an early years worker.

Five things to know about SEND

1) Children with SEND might have physical, communication and language, sensory, social and emotional, or intellectual needs, or they may have needs in one or more of these areas.
2) If children have been identified with SEND they may have an EHC plan to help staff plan for their needs.
3) All children should be given equal opportunities to participate when planning and carrying out activities in early years settings.
4) If children's needs require it they may be given one-to-one support by an adult.
5) You should read and be aware of the setting's policies.

Top marks

For this unit's assignment, you need to show that you can reflect on the role of the early years worker when meeting the individual needs of children aged 0–5 years.

List the requirements of the role of the early years worker when meeting the individual needs of children, saying why each one is important and giving examples of what might happen if it is not met effectively by staff.

Grading

In order to achieve assessment criteria 4.1 and also to achieve grading criteria D5 and A*, you will need to:

Identify ways to respond to the individual needs of children that treat children fairly and in line with current practice for diversity and inclusion.

Reflect on the role of the early years worker when meeting the individual needs of children aged from birth to five years.

Learning Outcome 5:
Know own preferred learning style and develop relevant study skills

When you start any kind of qualification or new learning, you will have your own responsibilities as a student. These will include organising your work and making sure that you understand and are clear about what you are learning, as well as keeping up to date with your studies. While you are studying for your qualification, it will help you if you can think about the way in which you learn best and how you should organise what you are doing.

High priority

How do you learn best? What motivates and inspires you to make the most of all your learning opportunities?

Assessment criteria grid

Learning outcomes	Assessment criteria
The learner will:	The learner can:
5. Know own preferred learning style and develop relevant study skills.	5.1. Reflect upon own preferred learning style.
	5.2. Identify relevant study skills.

5.1 Reflect upon own preferred learning style (D6)

Over the years, there has been plenty of wide-ranging psychological research into the way in which different people learn, and this has produced various learning style theories. These theories say that we all have different ways of learning, which affects the way in which we manage information, and that knowing about preferred learning styles will help both teachers and learners.

This learning aim asks you to think about the importance of knowing your own preferred learning style and the way in which you learn, so that you can plan your studies more effectively.

Learning styles have been divided into different types; some theories say that there are as many as seven while others prioritise three. For the purpose of this book, we have set out the three which are most often used when describing how people learn:

- visual learning style (learning through looking or seeing)
- auditory learning style (learning through hearing)
- tactile/kinaesthetic learning style (learning through touching and doing).

Visual learners have a strong focus on what they see, so are good at remembering what they read and write. They are able to understand

Do you know how you learn best?

information best when they see it, for example, through charts, pictures and presentations as well as printed information.

Auditory learners find that information is easier for them to take in and understand if they hear it. For example, when they are given instructions they will prefer to hear them rather than read them. Auditory learners may also say things out loud to help them to remember.

Tactile/kinaesthetic learners learn best through touching and doing. They prefer to learn in a practical way rather than by watching others and may find it difficult to take in information if they are simply listening. They may need to move around more than others to help them with their learning and have a shorter concentration span.

While this research has stated that there are several styles of learning, each individual person is complex and may find that they have a mixture of one or more of these. There are various tests which you can take online to help you to find out about the way in which you learn best, or you may know this already.

Extend

Outline three reasons why you think it is important for you to think about your own learning style.

Find out more about …

… research on learning theories by looking online and carry out a learning styles quiz, such as at www.educationplanner.org/students/self-assessments/learning-styles-quiz.shtml. Are you surprised by the results?

In addition to knowing your own learning style, it will help you to think about what motivates you when you are learning and how you approach it. We call these our metacognitive skills.

Tutors and teachers may talk to you about how you are going to approach your studies as part of their course induction at the start. This will be useful to look at alongside learning styles, because it encourages you to think about your strengths and weaknesses so that you can be more in control of what you are doing: this will help you to learn more.

Jargon buster

Metacognition – how we think about our learning, and our own awareness and knowledge of the process so that we can evaluate it.

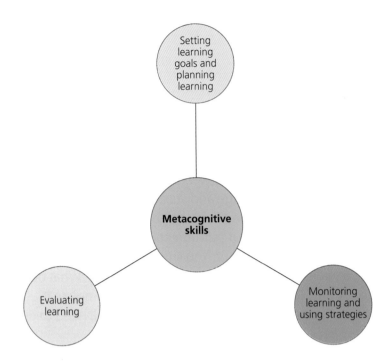

Setting learning goals and planning learning

Part of thinking about how we learn is to be able to set ourselves goals. These may be for the long or short term, and will help us to look at what we need to do to achieve them. For example, if you need to complete an assignment in the next four weeks, you can set a goal for yourself for each week so that you are planning and working towards completing it, rather than leaving it to the last minute or forgetting an important part of what is involved. Planning your learning may involve reading around what you need to do, checking the requirements of your assignment and thinking about the structure as well as finding a quiet time and place to write it. Remember when you are setting goals for yourself that they need to be attainable – in other words, you should be able to realistically achieve them.

Theory in action

Alexia has an assignment to write which needs to be handed in in three weeks' time. She knows that it will be her mum's birthday on the second weekend and that she will be spending that day with her family, and must set some time aside to buy a present. She also has to share the home computer with her twin brother but knows that he is out all day every Saturday at the football club.

- How could Alexia set herself goals in her situation so that she will be able to complete her assignment on time? Try to set some for her.
- Why might these restrictions make it easier for her to plan her assignment?

For more information on organising your learning, see section 5.2 on page 49.

Monitoring learning and using strategies that work for you

Monitoring your learning and using different strategies to help you will also support the way in which you learn and help you to be in control of your learning. Some of these strategies might be creating different ways of helping yourself based on what you know about your own learning:

- **Initiating your work** – sometimes the thought of starting is far worse than the task itself. If you know that it is a weakness of yours to leave things to the last minute, make a change and start the next task as soon as you can. You will feel a lot better and it will not be hanging over you.
- **Ask yourself questions** – this is about self-reflection and will be useful if you have a tendency to miss things out. You should ask yourself how you are doing and be able to look at your progress objectively. What do I know already about this? How can I organise my work to complete it effectively? What can I do if I get stuck? Is there anything I still need to do so that I can improve?
- **Use mnemonics** – you can use these to help you remember key points using the first letter of each aspect. For example, to help you remember the seven areas of learning and development, you may make up a sentence using the first letter of each area. Some people use the following mnemonic to help them remember the colours of the rainbow: 'Richard of York gave battle in vain' – red, orange, yellow, green, blue, indigo, violet.
- **Break into chunks to make it more manageable** – if you are revising and find it hard to work, try to set yourself goals so that you do not overstretch yourself by breaking it down into smaller chunks to help you. Then have a break and go back to it.
- **Check over your work** – this is always a good idea, particularly if you know that you tend to rush, as you may have missed things out.

You will probably think of other strategies as you study, but it is useful to keep this list close at hand while you are working so that you can look at them to help you and keep you focused on your learning.

Evaluating learning

Another important part of how we learn is to be able to evaluate it. This means we need to be able to look at what we have done and assess how we think it has gone. This may be after you have received feedback from an assignment, but you may also evaluate your learning by thinking about the progress you have made as you work. Self-assessment is an important part of learning as it focuses you on what has been asked and makes you think about how you have responded to it. It may help you to have a set of questions to help you to do this:

- What was I asked to do?
- Can I identify the key questions and have I covered all of them?

Activity

Based on what you know about your own learning, what kinds of learning strategies are helpful to you?

Extend

Investigate other strategies which may be useful.

- What have I learnt from this?
- What did I find easy/hard about it?
- Is there anything I could change/do differently?

5.2 Identify relevant study skills (D7, D8)

As well as knowing about the way in which you learn best, you will also
need to be familiar with a range of study skills which will help you to learn.
Remember that these are not specific to childcare but will be relevant to any
study situation. As you start to develop these skills you will find out what
works for you and what does not, so that you can find a way of meeting your
own needs. Study skills include:

- knowing how to organise yourself and how to manage your time
- where to find information to help you
- note-taking and note-making
- how to plan an assignment
- being able to reference and add a bibliography.

How does taking notes help you to learn?

Knowing how to organise yourself and how to manage your time

This is the first thing you need to think about when you are studying: each
person will find different ways which work for them. You will need to find
a suitable place where the things you need for study are close by – for

Get organised! Make sure you have a space that is your own to work in, preferably one that you do not need to move away from each time you finish studying. Think about getting your notes and learning materials ready so that you can make the most of the time that you have.

example, computer, books and writing materials. Your files and notes should be close by and you may want to label them clearly so that you can find things easily.

When thinking about how to manage your time, it might help you to look at your week and to identify different time slots which you can use to study. You should also consider how long you can study at any one time and what time of day is best for you to set aside to do it. If you have to share a family computer or study space, can you timetable it so that different people can use it at set times? Once you have done this, you will be able to develop your own timetable, making sure you have time to get out and do other things too as it is important to make time to do this.

Where to find information to help you

When you start to study, you will need to be able to find information from different places. These may be textbooks to start with but you will also be able to use the internet, newspapers and magazines as well as digital programmes such as podcasts and television programmes. Your teacher or tutor will probably give you a reading list of suggested sources for information but you may also like to find some of your own.

When you are using the internet for finding out information, you will need to be careful, particularly if you have used a search engine to find it. This is because although there is plenty of information on the internet, it might not come from a source which is trustworthy. One tip is to check that the domain name is a reliable source. For example, those which end in .gov. uk and .ac.uk can only come from educational and government sites, so will always be reliable sources. Your teacher or tutor may also give you a bibliography of reliable websites, books and magazine articles which may be useful to you when looking for information.

Jargon buster

Bibliography – a list of books or other sources of reference.

Note-taking and note-making

It might be helpful for you to make a distinction between these two to help you to think about how you use them.

● **Note-taking** – these are the notes you write down when you are listening to someone speaking. If you want to remember what they are saying, you should note down the most important (key) points, in a way which makes sense to you so that you can refer back to them. You should also remember to read through your notes soon after you have written them so that you can add to them and clarify anything which may be unclear to you later. Always use your own words to make notes, and if a word is used that you do not understand, underline it so that you can look it up later.

Read and write

You can practise taking notes in different contexts – watching a television programme or listening to a factual radio programme. Give yourself a limit of, say, ten minutes and see if you can make brief notes on the key points so that they make sense when you read them back.

- **Note-making** – this is when you write your own notes while reading through some text, which could be from a book, magazine or online article. When doing this, you need to be clear on why you are making the notes, so that you only write down what is relevant and useful. Keep the reason for the notes in your mind, or write them at the top of your note-making page, to help you to do this. If you can, it may help you to underline parts of text which may be useful the first time you read it. You must also make sure that you keep a record of the article or text so that you can reference it in your writing (see page 52 for more information on referencing).

Activity

Next time you have an assignment or activity to write, be sure to read through the points below to help you. Why is it important to organise yourself in this way?

How to plan an assignment

When you are asked to write an assignment for your course, you will need to plan it carefully.

1 Look very closely at what you are being asked about. You will need to make sure you understand what is being asked so that you can think about how you are going to structure what you say. If you have any questions about this for your teacher or tutor, make sure you ask them straight away.

2 Look very carefully at the command words to help you to answer the question; for example, whether you are being asked to 'describe', 'identify', 'reflect', 'explain', 'evaluate', and so on. Underline the key words to help you to focus on what is being asked.

3 Read around your subject and find out what you need to know, making notes and taking down your references as you go (see below on how to reference).

4 Plan your assignment, making sure you structure it carefully with an introduction, answering what has been asked and backing it up, and then finishing with a conclusion.

5 Make sure you relate what you have read in your research to what you have seen or what is in the task you have been given.

It may help you when planning your assignment to talk things through with your tutor

Unit 3 has more information to support you in this area, and to help you prepare for the multiple choice questions.

Being able to reference and add a bibliography

As a student, you will need to be able to reference so that you can show the person reading your work where you have found your information. This adds authenticity to what you are writing as well as showing to your tutor or teacher that you have read something around the subject. The most commonly used academic system for referencing is known as the Harvard System. In this system, the reference must contain the author's last name, the year of publication and the page number. If you are using books you will also need to add the publisher. However, you should check with your tutor that this is the system they want you to use. Your references should be clearly marked at the bottom of the page.

When you have finished a piece of work, you will also need to make sure that you add a bibliography at the end. A bibliography is a list of all the books and articles which you have referred to in your assignment.

It is important that we use references so that we acknowledge the ideas and contributions of others. If we use other's work without acknowledging it or saying where you have read it, this is known as plagiarism.

Jargon buster

Plagiarism – this means using or copying someone else's work and claiming that it is yours.

Copying the work of others is dishonest and can mean that you will be suspended from your course. This will depend on the measures taken by your school or college in these cases, but they are likely to take serious

Read and write

Find out more online about the Harvard referencing system and what it means. Have a go at referencing a page from a book so that you will know what to do more quickly.

measures if they find it has taken place. Plagiarism does not only mean copying from books, articles and the internet, but also copying from the assignments or work of others.

As well as making sure you develop self-awareness in your learning and finding out what works best for you when you are studying, you should also make the most of other help which will be available. This may be your teacher or tutor, librarian or a study or discussion group which may help and motivate you. Remember also that others in your class or group or those who have studied the subject in the past may also have found useful sources of information which they may be able to share with you.

Five things to know about how you learn and study best

1) Develop an awareness of your learning style and the way you learn and use this to help you.
2) Recognise your own strengths and weaknesses so that you know what to focus on.
3) Try to organise your studies as much as you can, as you can then make the most of your time and set yourself goals and opportunities for review.
4) Acknowledge and reference any reading which you have done to help you.
5) Make the most of any help from others which is available to support you in your studies.

My life as a student

'When I first started my childcare qualification I hadn't really been into studying anything before. But because I was really interested in what I was doing, it suddenly became very important to me to do everything well. I bought lots of new files and stationery – this helped motivate me to study and also made the qualification more special. Then I made sure I had a really nice space for study that was set up so that I wasn't distracted by anything. I found out that I am a visual learner so I need peace and quiet as well as nice surroundings. So far it's going really well and I am finding the studying easier than I thought I would at the start.'

Roxi, early years student

Grading

In order to achieve assessment criteria 5.1 and 5.2 and also to achieve grading criteria D6, D7 and D8, you will need to:

Reflect on the importance of knowing your own learning style.

Identify different study skills needed to study effectively.

Include at least one reference and a bibliography.

Unit 2

Development and well-being 0–5 years

About this unit

Everyone who works with children has to know about how the growth and development of children. In this unit we look at the patterns of children's development and how to observe development. We also look at factors that might affect development both positively and negatively. In this unit, you will also learn about how everyday activities and routines can support children's development. Finally, we also look at how changes in children's routines and lives can affect development, and ways in which early years settings can support children's routines.

Learning Outcome 1: Understand the expected pattern of holistic child development

Assessment criteria grid

Learning outcomes The learner will:	Assessment criteria The learner can:
1 Understand the expected pattern of holistic child development.	1.1 Describe the expected pattern of children's development from 0–5 years and include: physical development language development intellectual development social and emotional development

High priority

Make sure you have learnt what is in each of the four areas of development.

You need to understand how each area supports children's development.

Check you understand how the areas of development link together.

For each area of development, learn the patterns of development for different ages of children.

One of the amazing things about young children is the way that they grow and develop so quickly. In this section, we will look at how children typically develop at different ages. We will also consider why it is important for early years workers to know about children's pattern of development.

1.1. Describe the expected pattern of children's development from 0–5 years

Children's development is a huge topic area. This is why it is often split into different areas. We will divide it into four areas:

- physical development
- language development
- intellectual development
- social and emotional development.

The table on page 56 gives an overview of what is in each area.

An overview of each area of development

Physical development	Movement, balance and co-ordination
Language development	Talking, listening and understanding Reading and writing for older children
Intellectual development	Thinking, memory and understanding concepts such as time, colour and number
Social and emotional development	Relationships with others, managing feelings, confidence and self-control

Check what you know

What are the four areas of development? See if you can write them as a list.

Physical development

Physical development is about the movements that children make. It also relates to the skills that allow movement to take place such as balance, muscle strength and co-ordination. We will be looking at physical development in more depth later on.

Extend

Start watching the way that children walk and run. Notice how younger children are slower and their movements are not as smooth.

What physical skills are these children learning?

Language development

Language development is about how children are able to talk, listen but also communicate by pointing and using facial expressions. This is an area of development that helps children to play with others, express their needs and also understand what is happening. By four years, most children are able to talk and listen well, but at first babies rely on crying and using **facial expressions** to communicate with adults. When children go to school, language development also includes learning to read and write.

Jargon buster

Facial expressions – using the face to communicate by smiling or frowning, for example.

Activity

Make a list of how you have used your language development so far today.

- Who have you talked to?
- Have you listened to the radio?
- Has someone spoken to you?
- Did you use any body language?
- How has being able to communicate and understand helped you today?

Intellectual development

Intellectual development is about how we think, learn, remember and use information. It is sometimes known as cognitive development. There are many skills within intellectual development such as the ability to solve problems, put things into categories (organising things so that we can make sense of them) and think about things such as number. A good example of a skill involving intellectual development is doing a jigsaw puzzle. It requires thinking about the shape of the pieces and also being logical.

Theory in action

Max is ten months old. He watches as his dad pulls out a bib from the drawer. Max crawls towards his highchair without his dad saying anything. His dad lifts him into his highchair and then starts to feed him.

- Why did Max crawl to the highchair?
- What has Max learnt and remembered about the bib?
- Why is this an example of intellectual development?

This baby has learnt to drop things over the side of the highchair. Why is this an example of intellectual development?

Social and emotional development

Social and emotional development are often put together as they are very closely linked.

Social development is about children learning to be with others and understand what others might be thinking. It is mainly about how well we can make relationships with others. It involves skills such as sharing and taking turns, but also thinking about what others might be feeling. As part of social development, children have to learn to behave according to the social situation that they are in. This may mean sitting when eating or being quiet in a train.

Emotional development is about how we feel about ourselves and how we learn to control our emotions. At first young children find it hard to control their emotions. Two-year-olds will often have tantrums but a few minutes later, they may find something very funny. Emotional development is also about how we come to think about ourselves. How confident we feel is linked to emotional development. The link between emotional and social development is strong. This is because children who feel happy and confident find it easier to make friends.

Activity

Being able to understand others is part of social development.

- What are the signs that someone is annoyed with you?
- How did you learn to recognise these signs?

Development is holistic

One of the interesting things about children's development is the way each area of development is linked to others. If children have a problem in one area of development, it can affect others. The term '**holistic**' is used when talking about children's development to explain how different areas of development come together.

Let's look at how the different areas of development link to each other.

Jargon buster

Holistic development – children's overall development.

Physical development

Children's physical development affects other areas. A toddler who can now walk is able to move around. This means that the toddler can now see and touch new things. This in turn means that the toddler is learning more. It also means that the adult with the toddler is likely to name the objects and talk to the toddler about them. This now means that the toddler is able to learn new words and so the toddler's language development is helped.

Activity

Maisie is three years old. Her stage of development means that she can now play co-operatively with other children. Maisie has one friend that loves playing with dough. Maisie did not usually like to play with this, but now she often joins her friend and is learning to roll and cut the dough. When she and her friends play, they often use words or expressions that later Maisie copies.

- Describe how Maisie's ability to play with others is helping her learn new physical skills.
- Describe how Maisie is learning new words.

Language development

Children's language development is linked to many areas of development. Language helps children to understand and communicate with others. This means that it is closely linked to children's social and emotional development. Once children are talking fairly well at around three years, we can see that the way they play with others changes. They are likely to take turns and be more co-operative.

Language development is also linked to children's ability to learn and think in complex ways. This is because we often use language to help us think. Most people have an 'inner voice' that helps them to think about things or reminds them to do things. When you are very busy and alone, you may find that you talk aloud.

Young children often talk aloud when they are playing, as a way of helping them to organise themselves or their play.

Intellectual development

Intellectual development is important to many areas of development. This is because it is about learning, thinking and remembering. A baby might learn that by waving their fist, they can make a rattle shake and so practise the movement and help their physical development.

Children's social development is also linked to how well children can learn and think. A three-year-old may be told by other children that she cannot play with them because she ran off with the ball. She thinks about this and gives the ball back so that she can play with them. She has used her intellectual skills to analyse the situation and to work out what she should do.

Language and intellectual development are closely linked as we have seen. Children who have difficulty with language may find it hard to use and develop their intellectual skills or, on the other hand, they might not be able to communicate their ideas and thoughts. This in turn can make children feel very frustrated.

Social and emotional development

Humans are social beings. This means that social and emotional development are important in daily life. By being with others, children learn a variety of skills and ideas. A good example of this would be a child who wants to play with other children who are playing on a climbing frame. The child starts to climb so that she can join them.

Children's emotional development is also important to other areas of development. Children who feel good about themselves and are confident are more likely to try out new things and persist. This means that they can learn more. This is often referred to as **resilience**.

Measuring development

In order to describe the pattern of children's development, early years workers and other professionals look at a range of skills or **milestones** in each of the areas of development. These milestones are significant as they are typically seen at certain ages. A good example of a milestone is talking. When a child says his or her first word, this is a milestone. Most children start to say their first words at around 15 months as this is the usual pattern of development for language.

We will look at some of the important milestones for children of different ages later on. For your course, you will need to know these.

Differences between children's development

While early years workers need to know about typical patterns of children's development, children are not made in factories and no child is the same as another! This means that some children reach different milestones more quickly than others. A good example of this is walking. While most children are walking by 15 months, some children will start before they are one year old and others will be 18 months. There are many reasons why children's development may vary. We look at factors affecting development in Learning Outcome 3 of this unit, page 101.

Why early years workers learn about child development

There are many practical reasons why it is important to know about how children develop. Here are four important ones:
● To plan activities – what children need to learn and what they can do will depend on their age and stage of development. Early years workers need to know this in order to plan activities and play experiences.

Why did the early years worker need to plan this activity according to the development of this child?

- To plan routines – children's physical needs change according to their age and stage. Early years workers need to know about typical development in order to plan routines.
- To understand why children do things – children respond differently according to their stage of development. Babies, for example put things in their mouths as a way of exploring while two-year-olds find it hard to share things. If early years workers understand what is typical at different ages and stages, it can help them to respond correctly to the situation.
- To recognise when children need help – some children may need more help to support their development than others. They may have difficulties in learning or with mobility. Perhaps they will need to be seen by other professionals. When early years workers recognise that a child is not following the usual pattern of development, they can take steps to help the child.

Theory in action

Alice is three years old. Typically most children at three years talk using simple sentences, and what they say is fairly clear. When Alice talks, adults and other children find it hard to understand her. She does not say many words and is not making sentences.

Alice has just started at a pre-school. Her early years worker has recognised that Alice might need more help. The early years worker has arranged for Alice and her parents to meet a speech and language therapist. The early years worker is also planning activities that will encourage Alice to talk more.

- Explain how the early years worker is using her knowledge of the patterns of child development to work effectively with Alice.

Five things to know about children's development

1) Children's development can be split into four areas.
2) Each area of development is linked to the other areas of development.
3) Holistic development is the term used when talking about children's overall development.
4) Development is measured by professionals by looking at milestones or patterns of development.
5) Children can develop at different rates at their own individual pace.

An overview of children's development

Before looking in detail at children's development, let's look at the general picture of children's development according to their age.

Pattern of development from birth to one year

In the first year of life, babies make huge leaps in their development. There are milestones for every three months as it is possible to see clear developmental progress in most areas during this time.

Some of the most significant development is within their physical development. Babies go from having no control over their legs and arms to being able to pick things up, feed themselves and to being able to move. They also become physically much stronger as at first, they are unable to hold their heads up.

In this year, babies also move from just crying when they are newborn to being able to make babbling and tuneful sounds. They also learn how to get the attention of adults by smiling and laughing as well as pointing at objects. What is also amazing is that in this year babies have started to work out some of what their parents and key carers say to them.

Pattern of development from one to two years

In this period, babies continue to make rapid progress with their physical development. They are likely to walk in the first few months of this year and learn to move around. As this takes practice and some skill, this age group is often known as 'toddlers' because of the way that they move.

Children in this period are likely to increasingly understand what is said to them. By the time they reach two years, they should be able to say at least 50 recognisable words.

Toddlers like being next to other children, but do not typically play with them. They are happier playing with adults and prefer to stay close to their parents or key carers. Toddlers are keen to explore and quickly work out how to open things, including doors.

Check what you know

Look at the pattern of development for toddlers aged 1–2 years. Make a list of the areas of development and then write the skills that toddlers typically show in each area.

Pattern of development from two to three years

This is a very interesting year in children's overall development. Children's movement becomes more co-ordinated and they are increasingly independent. Most children in this year will move out of nappies and also be able to do some simple dressing. Children's ability to balance, throw and use wheeled toys also improves.

During this year, children's language develops quickly. Children move from joining two words together to being able to put simple sentences together. They learn to use simple questions and quickly pick up new words.

For many parents and key carers, it is children's emotional and social development that causes challenges. This age is very impulsive and determined. For example, children may find it hard to understand why they cannot have everything and do everything they want to do, at the very moment when they feel they want to! Frustration can lead to tantrums. As part of typical development, children will often want to be with other children but they do not usually have the social skills to be able to take turns, share and be co-operative. This can cause many arguments as they snatch things from each other and are less tolerant with each other than older children tend to be.

What is a common cause of tantrums in two-year-olds?

Read and write

Create a leaflet that shows parents/key carers some typical patterns of development for children aged 0–1, 1–2 and 2–3 years. Where possible, use photographs/drawings to illustrate the pattern of development.

Pattern of development from three to five years

During these years, children's social and emotional development leads the way as friendships and being with children of a similar age becomes important to them The turning point comes at three when children are usually able to be co-operative with other children. At first, this is for short periods, but by the time children reach five years, they can play together for several hours. It is also interesting to see that as children become four and older, they tend to play and have strong friendships with children of the same gender.

One of the reasons why children are more co-operative is that they are usually talking and understanding well. Most children will become fluent in language at four years.

Children in this age group are also showing significant steps in their intellectual development. This is linked to their language development, but also because of physical changes and growth in the brain. Children are often able to name colours and do simple jigsaw puzzles, and are able to do some problem-solving and reasoning. At five years, most children are counting objects and also starting to learn to read.

What skills do these children have that allow them to play together?

The expected pattern of physical development

Physical development is the range of movements and skills that children will learn in their first few years of life. Physical development is important to children's holistic development because being able to move, balance and use hands allows children to play. It also lets children become independent as they learn to feed and dress themselves.

Fine and gross motor movements

Physical development is usually divided into two further areas:

- **fine motor movements**
- **gross motor movements**.

Actions requiring fine and gross motor movements

Fine motor movements	Gross motor movements
Using a pencil to draw or write with	Kicking a ball
Turning pages in a book	Jumping from a step
Tying shoelaces	Climbing
Using a zip	Using a tricycle

Combined movements

While fine motor and gross motor movements are looked at separately, many tasks require both types of movements. A good example of this is putting on a pair of trousers. Putting a leg into the trouser is a gross motor movement, but pulling up the trousers and doing up a zip is a fine motor movement.

Categorising skills

Fine motor movements	Gross motor movements

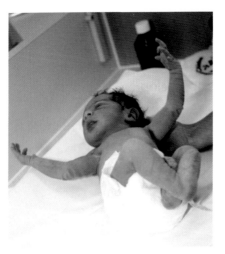

Newborns are born with a range of survival reflexes

Pattern of physical development: birth to one year

Physical development is a key area in the first year of a baby's life. This is because at first babies are helpless and dependent on their key carer, and in order to survive, they need to learn to become mobile. Babies are born with a range of reflex movements that will help them to survive. Some of them are obvious such as being able to cry, suck and breathe. There are other reflexes too which disappear as the baby gains more control over his or her body.

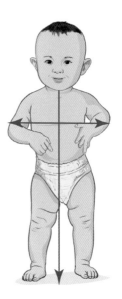

Activity

Using an internet search engine or a child development reference book, find out about two other reflex movements that newborns show:

- moro reflex
- grasp reflex.

One of the earliest movements that babies learn is to lift and control movement of their head. It has been recognised that babies follow a pattern of gaining control over their bodies. You can learn this as two words: downwards and outwards.

- **Downwards** – control is gained firstly downwards, with babies learning to move their heads before their arms and then their legs.
- **Outwards** – babies also gain control outwards. This means that they learn to master using their arms before gaining control over their hands.

Learning to move

By the end of a baby's first year, they will be crawling or moving in some way. They should also be able to pull themselves up to standing. Some babies may even be walking. Learning to move follows a pattern with babies sitting up before crawling, standing and then walking. To be able to move, babies need to develop strength and co-ordination.

Fine motor skills

In the first year, babies also start to co-ordinate their hand movements. They learn to pass objects from one hand to the other and also to put down or drop objects. By the end of the first year, most babies can use their hands to feed themselves and can also pick up small objects using their thumbs and first fingers. This movement is called a pincer grasp.

Movement milestones during the baby's first year

Age	Fine motor movements	Gross motor movements
3 months	Clasps and unclasps hands	Moves head to watch things
6 months	Can pass a toy from one hand to another Can reach and grasp toys	Can sit up with support Can roll from front to back
9 months	Can hold and bite bread crust Puts hand around cup or bottle Can use rattle or shaker	Can sit up alone Attempts to crawl Stands holding on
12 months	Points using index finger to objects Can pass a toy to an adult and release it	Stands and can walk holding on to furniture

How is the baby using a physical skill to help communication?

Extend

Tummy time

Find out why babies are meant to spend time on their tummies.

Look at this weblink to find out how tummy time helps babies' physical development:

www.firstcommunityhealthcare.co.uk/sites/default/files/pl-469-2-babies-and-tummy-time.pdf

Pattern of physical development: one to two years

Between the ages of one and two, nearly all babies learn to walk and also how to sit down after standing. The term 'toddler' is used for children when they first walk as they are quite unsteady and often have to put their arms out.

From around 18 months most toddlers can also crawl upstairs and then crawl down bottom first. They also start to move more quickly, although they often find it hard to avoid obstacles.

Toddlers also start to co-ordinate their hand movements. During this year, they learn to use a spoon to feed themselves, although this can be quite messy. They also learn how to drink from a beaker.

Toddlers also enjoy using toys such as bricks and carrying things.

Movement milestones during the first and second year

Age	Fine motor movements	Gross motor movements
1–2 years	Picks up objects between thumb and finger – pincer grasp Can use spoon to feed Can hold a cup and drink from it	From 18 months is walking well Enjoys climbing into low chairs Pushes or pulls toys on floor

How can learning to feed and drink help this child's emotional development?

Pattern of physical development: two to three years

This is a year when children's physical development really develops. They become more co-ordinated and so are able to show many skills. Children are able to run, jump and climb. This age group is known for being restless and active.

Two-year-olds' fine motor skills are still developing, but they are able to do more movements involving the hands, including using a spoon and fork and also some simple dressing. This is also the year when children start to use the toilet rather than nappies.

Movement milestones during the second and third year

Age	Fine motor movements	Gross motor movements
2–3 years	Uses a spoon to feed independently Develops a preferred hand for holding pencils and other objects Can build a tower of seven or more cubes Can make circular marks and also lines with pencil or paints	Walks upstairs one foot joining the other Climbs climbing frame Can throw ball Can ride tricycle and steer it Can kick a ball gently

Pattern of children's physical development: three to five years

Over these years, children become increasingly skilled and fast in their gross motor movements. Some children may start to use bicycles while others may begin to swim. Children are often able to run, jump and throw with ease. They are also able to avoid obstacles.

Children's fine motor skills are also developing. By the end of this period, children can dress themselves apart from doing up zips and laces. They are also able to eat using a spoon and fork or other cutlery used in their family. Children are also able to play with toys that require hand strength and co-ordination, such as lego or jigsaws.

Movement milestones for three to five years

Age	Fine motor movements	Gross motor movements
3	Can build a tower of 9 cubes Threads large wooden beads Holds pencil in preferred hand Cuts with scissors	Jumps from low step, two feet together Walks up and downstairs, one foot to each stair Can steer tricycle and manage corners
4	Can use a spoon and fork well to eat Can dress and undress but not laces, button or zips Can thread small beads Can use jigsaws and toys with small parts	Can sit with knees crossed Can stand and run on tiptoe Can bounce and catch a large ball
5	Can thread a large needle and sew large stitches Can copy name and write simple words Can colour in shapes Can use scissors to cut on line	Can walk on a narrow line Can stand on one foot Can skip and move rhythmically to music Can hop on each foot

The importance of early years workers understanding the pattern of physical development

If adults understand how children develop gross motor skills and learn to walk, they can help children by providing them with the right opportunities. Adults can help babies and children by giving them opportunities to move and explore. Too much time spent sitting, such as in a pushchair, can be a problem for children's physical development.

In the first year, babies need time on the floor on their tummies so that their muscles can develop. Later, babies need safe opportunities to learn to stand and walk by holding on to furniture or an adult's hand.

Older children need plenty of space to learn to run, climb, kick and throw. This is why going to the park or playing outdoors is important. Adults who understand the stage of development of an individual child will be able to provide the right equipment such as tricycles, balls and bats at the right time. This will allow older children to learn the skills needed to play with them.

If adults understand the pattern of physical development, they will know that the development of hand–eye co-ordination takes time. They will know that children need encouragement and activities that are at the right level for their stage of development. One of the ways that children can learn to control their hands is by doing everyday things for themselves, and adults can support this. Feeding and dressing are great ways for children to learn to use their hands. At first children can be very slow, but over time they do learn the skills they need. As well as giving opportunities for everyday skills, children can also benefit from playing with toys as well as opportunities to draw, paint and use materials such as dough, sand and water.

Check what you know

Make a list of ways in which adults can help children's physical development.

Patterns of language development

Language development is about the skills required to express yourself and understand others. This includes pointing, smiling but also talking and listening. Learning to talk and understand takes quite a while with most children not talking well until they are around four years old. This is because learning to talk is a difficult task. Children have to learn that sounds stand for words and also that there is a way of putting words together.

Some children will also be learning more than one language. This means that they have to learn the sounds for each language and also the different ways in which the words go together to make sentences.

Learning to talk, listen and understand are important skills in helping children to make relationships, play with others and also to think.

Language is often divided into two skills:

- **receptive language** – this is what babies and children can understand
- **expressive language** – this is what babies and children can say

Jargon buster

Receptive language – the words and sentences that babies and children can understand.

Expressive language – the sounds, words and sentences that babies and children can say.

Check what you know

Can you explain the difference between receptive language and expressive language? See if you can give an example of each in everyday life.

Why do children need receptive and expressive language in order to play together?

Pattern of language development: birth to one year

Babies learn to communicate quickly but without using any words! At first they cry, but then within a few weeks, they make cooing sounds and learn to smile. Babies also learn to recognise faces and also tones of voice. This means that they often start to cry if they hear angry voices or see an angry face.

Understanding language takes a lot longer. This year is sometimes called pre-linguistic as babies are not able to say words, although they may start to recognise the meanings of a few words from around nine months. Interestingly, babies in this year start to make sounds. The sounds are called babbling. Babbling changes over the year to sound more like the language that the adults around them are using.

Language milestones from birth to one year

Age	Expressive language	Receptive language
6 weeks	Coos	Recognises parent's voice and calms down if crying Turns to look at speaker's face
3 months	Makes happy sounds when spoken to	Can be soothed quickly when adult talks and holds baby
6 months	Babbles with repeated sounds, dah-dah Laughs and chuckles when happy	Turns to look at parent if hears voice across the room
9 months	Makes sounds to gain attention Babbling becomes longer and baby will babble when alone	Understands 2 or 3 phrases used frequently by adults, e.g. 'no' and 'bye-bye'
12 months	Babbling is tuneful and in long strings Raises voice to gain attention	Can follow simple instructions, e.g. give me the spoon Understands words used frequently in routines, e.g. 'cup', 'spoon', 'go for a walk'

Read and write

Language milestones birth to one year

Create a leaflet for a new parent that identifies the language milestones for a baby's first year of life.

Pattern of language development: one to two years

During this year, children start to understand more of what is being said and they will start to use words although they will continue to babble. The words that toddlers use will reflect what happens in their daily lives but also what is important to them.

Toddlers will also use one word to mean several things. 'Dink' might refer to a toddler wanting more drink, but also more food, or a cup.

By the time children reach two years, most children should have at least 50 words and will be starting to put two words together, for example, 'more dink'.

Language milestones from one to two years

Age	Expressive language	Receptive language
15 months	Continues to babble Uses 2–6 words	Understands many words Can follow a simple instruction of three or four words – 'Give me the ball'
18 months	Talks using babbling and different sounds when alone Uses 6–20 words When adults talk, toddlers will often echo back last word	Enjoys looking at books and pointing to pictures Understands instructions and simple conversations Enjoys hearing and tries to join in nursery rhymes
2 years	Uses 50 or more words Puts two words together to make simple sentences Refers to self by name Talks to self Echoes back words when adults are talking	Carries out a simple instruction which may have many words – 'Tell Mandy that lunch is ready' Can point to several parts of the body Understands a wide range of words

Check what you know

Which of these statements about children's language development aged one to two years are true?

- Most children at 15 months are able to say at least 20 words.
- Most children at 18 months are babbling as well as saying a few words.
- Most children at two years are able to point to parts of the body.

Pattern of language development: two to three years

During this year, children's language develops very quickly. They start the year having 50 or so words, but by three years, they will be using sentences and questions. Children in this period also learn to use language to gain an adult's attention. They may repeatedly use 'what's dat?' to engage an adult in conversation, or use an adult's name to gain attention. During this year, children's speech can be hard to understand unless the adult knows the child well, as their speech sounds are still developing.

By three years, most of what children say can be understood by adults, although not every word or sound will be clear. In this period, some children may also stutter at times. This is more likely when children are anxious or excited.

Language milestones from two to three years

Age	Expressive language	Receptive language
2 years 6 months	200 or more words Knows full name Constantly asking simple questions such as 'what' and 'where' May stutter Knows and says a few rhymes	Enjoys simple books Knows and recognises a few rhymes Understands most of what adults say to him or her Is starting to follow an instruction with two parts, e.g. 'Get your toothbrush and bring it here'
3 years	Asks many questions beginning with 'what', 'why' and 'who' Speech is more tuneful Large vocabulary Uses 'I', 'me', 'he' and 'him' Most of what is said can be understood by others	Listens to stories and enjoys sharing books Can follow instructions in two parts, e.g. 'Find Teddy's hat and put it on him'

How do these children's language skills help them to learn more?

Pattern of language development: three to five years

During these two years children become fluent in their language, and by four years most children can talk about events in the past and future.

Children also use their language to be more co-operative. While children will still squabble over toys and activities, it is interesting to see that instead of pushing or snatching, most children will start to use language to make their point: 'If you don't let me have it, I will tell on you!'

Children are also able to use their language to explain their actions and give their point of view. The increase in children's language during this time also helps their behaviour. They can understand the reasons for rules, and also use language to understand concepts such as 'later' or 'now'. Children with lower levels of language will often find it harder to play with others, and may show more bursts of unwanted behaviour.

Table showing language milestones at 4 and 5 years

Age	Expressive	Receptive
4 years	Children can be understood easily by others Most of what they say is grammatically correct Loves asking questions Enjoys telling stories	Enjoys hearing jokes, especially ones with sounds Knows several nursery rhymes Can pick out rhymes Loves hearing stories and sharing books
5 years	Often asks the meanings of words or the word for an object Loves using words accurately and will correct others, e.g. 'That's not a shoe, that's a boot!' Argues and squabbles using language	Loves hearing and making up jokes Can pick out individual sounds in words (important for learning to read)

Theory in action

Maddie is four years old. She loves to play with her friends and together they spend a lot of time talking as they play. She knows several nursery rhymes that she often sings, even when she is by herself. Her parents have noticed that she is starting to argue back when it is bed time or if she is asked to do something that she does not like. She also squabbles with her older brother, and has started to make up jokes.

- Explain which aspects of Maddie's language development are typical.
- Are there any aspects of Maddie's language that are advanced or delayed?
- Describe how Maddie's language supports other areas of her development.

The importance of understanding the pattern of children's language development

Language development is interesting because it is strongly linked to how well adults work with children. Adults who can recognise the stage of children's language development can work in ways that will help children to make progress. There are many skills that adults need to show with children of different ages and stages.

Babies and toddlers

- **Talking and listening** – adults need to be good at gently talking to babies and toddlers. They need to leave time for babies and toddlers to respond. This is important because babies and toddlers need to feel that they are part of the conversation, even if they are just babbling.

- **Eye contact and pointing** – adults also need to make eye contact with the babies and toddlers as seeing an adult's face helps with understanding. In order for babies and toddlers to understand the meaning of words, adults need to point or show the baby or toddler what they are talking about.
- **Books and rhymes** – babies and toddlers can also be helped if adults show them books and sing rhymes to them. Babies and toddlers like to hear repeated sentences and songs. Repetition seems to help them master the meanings of words.

How can sharing a book support this child's language development?

Read and write

Create a leaflet to help parents understand the importance of talking to their baby. You can gain additional information by visiting the Literacy Trust website and looking at the section 'Talk to your Baby': www. literacytrust.org.uk/talk_to_your_baby/resources.

From two to five years

- **Being responsive** – once children are starting to talk, it is important that adults are good at listening to them and taking an interest in what they say. This skill is often called 'being responsive'. Adults who are responsive find that children tend to talk more to them. As progress in language is linked to how often children talk, this means that children who have plenty of time chatting with an adult tend to do well.
- **Doing interesting things** – children also learn language when they are doing things with adults or playing with interesting things. This is because children naturally want to talk about something that is exciting or fascinating. The role of the adult is to be responsive and also to use the correct words for objects and actions, for example, 'Let's crack open the egg.'

● **Books and rhymes** – books are also important for children's language. This is because children get plenty of time with an adult when sharing a book, and also because books often introduce children to new words. Books that repeat or have rhymes are particularly popular at first. Later, as children's language develops, they tend to like books that have a story.

Patterns of intellectual development

Intellectual development is a collection of skills including memory, thinking, understanding and using information, and problem-solving. The development of these skills allows children to learn about concepts such as time, space and mathematics. Children's intellectual development is very variable and depends on the experiences that they have, how well adults talk to them and also their language development. This means that, unlike other areas of development, there are fewer milestones that can be easily picked out.

Pattern of intellectual development: birth to one year

During their first year, babies start to learn about how the world around them looks. It is highly stimulating as everything is new. It takes time for babies to understand what they are seeing because while the eye sends images to the brain, the brain has to work out what they mean.

Similarly, babies have to learn what noises mean and over the next few months, they will learn to recognise that certain sounds are linked to daily routines, such as running a bath. They will also learn to associate certain sounds as being words.

It is thought that one of the reasons that babies sleep so much is because their brains have to work so hard to figure out what is happening. An interesting milestone in intellectual development is when babies start to realise that when objects are out of sight they still exist. This understanding is known as 'object permanence'.

Intellectual milestones from birth to one year

Age	Intellectual development
0–3 months	Learns to see all of the colours – at birth it is thought that they can only see in shades of black and white
	Can focus on objects held close
	Notices when objects are moving
3–6 months	Recognises familiar faces – thus using their memory
	Starts to notice and interpret people's facial expressions
	Recognises and thus remembers familiar sounds
6–9 months	Can recognise when things are far away
	Intrigued when things appear to be strange or impossible, e.g. things that dangle in mid-air
	Remembers simple games and will show excitement
9–12 months	Develops object permanence
	Shows interest in simple puzzles, e.g. pop-up toys
	Remembers how simple toys work

What has this child understood about objects that are out of sight?

Pattern of intellectual development: one to two years

In this year, babies start to walk and move around. Their fine motor skills are also developing and so they are able to learn and explore more easily.

Children will not plan their movements ahead, but instead will learn by seeing what happens. This is sometimes called **'trial by error'** learning. A good example of this is discovering what happens when items drop – they will often drop items from highchairs and pushchairs to watch how they fall down.

Toddlers' ability to judge time, speed and distance is still developing, and so they are likely to walk into or even over objects. In this year, many toddlers learn the link between words and pictures. This means that they will often point to a favourite picture or book if an adult asks them. When children are nearly two years old, they start to understand that if they look in a mirror, they are seeing themselves looking back. Up until this point, children often think that they are looking at another baby or child.

Intellectual milestones from one to two years

Age	Intellectual development
1–2 years	Points to a named picture
	Remembers simple games
	Remembers how to push buttons on toys to make sounds or lights flash
	Understands that it is their own reflection in a mirror

Pattern of intellectual development: two to three years

In this period, children's language is developing quickly, which means that they are able to plan a little more. A child may wait for an adult to be out of a room before doing something!

Language also helps children to categorise objects. Children may start to accurately say things such as 'Nanny's dog', instead of everything with four legs being a dog. They are also able to notice differences in sizes and can start to understand terms such as 'big' or 'little'.

Most children in this year will also start to enjoy simple puzzles, although they may need help with ones that are complicated. Most of their learning takes place when they are busy exploring and playing. This is because most children of this age are very active and find sitting still difficult.

Intellectual milestones from two to three years

Age	Intellectual development
2–3 years	Can manage a simple puzzle of 3 pieces
	Copies a circle
	Can point to a 'little' teddy or a 'big' teddy
	Can stack beakers in order
	Can match three colours

Pattern of intellectual development: three to five years

Between three and five years, children show huge strides in their intellectual development. This happens gradually and is linked to how their language has developed and how adults work with them. Children who have adults around to explain what they are seeing or encourage them to ask questions are likely to make more progress.

Children also need plenty of opportunities to experience using different materials and seeing different things. This allows them to make connections and to think.

By the time most children are five years old, they can count, talk about size and also use some strategies to solve some practical problems.

Intellectual milestones from three to five years

Age	Intellectual development
3–4 years	Tells if an object is heavy Matches one to one, e.g. putting a cup with each saucer Knows red, blue and green Is able to sort simple objects, e.g. put all the blue buttons in one place or separate cars from lorries
4–5 years	Picks up a number of objects (up to ten), e.g. 'Find me four cars' Names times of day associated with different activities, e.g. bedtime Matches symbols, e.g. letters and numbers Can count to 20 Plans what to play with Understands that there are rules and can explain them to other children

Which skills are needed to complete a jigsaw puzzle?

Why early years workers need to understand the pattern of intellectual development

If adults understand how children's intellectual development progresses, they can plan activities and experiences that will support children.

Interestingly, children's intellectual development is linked to the amount of stimulation that is provided for them. Stimulation can happen when children are talking with adults but also when they are doing interesting things.

Some of the best stimulation takes place when there is a combination of both talk and activity. This is because, as we have seen, language and intellectual development are closely linked. Activities that work well for all ages include cooking, going for a walk and meal times. Adults who understand the pattern of children's intellectual development understand that children's language also plays a part in their intellectual development. They will also recognise when and how to teach children concepts such as number.

Activity

Jasmine is two-and-a-half years old. She is an active child but her language has been slow to develop. She can complete a simple jigsaw and can tell the difference between a big cuddly toy and a small one. Her mother has been trying to teach her to do simple sums using flashcards. Jasmine has not been interested. Her mother is worried that Jasmine may have problems learning. She has asked an early years worker for their opinion.

- Identify whether Jasmine's development seems typical.
- Explain why she may not be ready for flashcards and sums.
- Suggest an activity that might help Jasmine's intellectual development.

Patterns of social and emotional development

Social and emotional development are two areas of development that are closely linked. This is why they are often grouped together.

- Social development is about the relationships that we have with others and also how we fit into groups.
- Emotional development is about our feelings and also our identity.

Children's social and emotional development is important because they need to learn to get along with others and also to understand and control their feelings.

Check what you know

Can you explain the difference between social and emotional development?

Pattern of social and emotional development: birth to one year

Babies are born to be social. Within a few minutes of being born, they gaze into the eyes of their parents. The terms '**attachment**' and '**bonding**' are used to describe how babies and their parents build a loving relationship. This relationship is important and how well it develops affects children's later emotional development. Children who develop a strong bond with their parents and key carer find it easier to trust others and also to care about other people.

The attachment/bond between parents and key carer is developed in many ways, but particularly through physical contact and soothing talk. Being held and talked to helps babies feel loved and also encourages them to communicate. While most parents feel protective and have a strong bond towards their baby, at first babies can be handled and calmed down by anyone. This changes in the first year so that by nine months, babies start to actively want to be with their parents/key carer.

Jargon buster

Attachment – the process by which children and their parents develop a strong loving relationship.

Bonding – the process by which children and their parents develop a strong loving relationship.

Social and emotional milestones from birth to one year

Age	Social development	Emotional development
0–3 months	Watches parents face Smiles and coos	Cries to show distress Will calm down when hears parent's voice
6 months	Responds to faces and tones of voice	Screams with annoyance Enjoys being with parents and family members
9 months	Laughs and enjoys being played with	Is unsure about strangers Shows preference to be with parents or key carer
12 months	Enjoys playing simple games such as peek-a-boo	Cries if cannot see parent or key carer

Theory in action

Ahmed is nearly a year old. His parents have noticed a change in him. When he was younger, he was happy to be cuddled by his grandparents when they visited every few weeks. Now when his grandmother picks him up, he cries and turns to his mother. His parents are worried that he might have a shy personality.

- Identify Ahmed's stage of emotional development.
- Explain why Ahmed used to be happy to be cuddled by his grandparents but cries now.
- If Ahmed's grandparents visited him every day, would his behaviour change?

Pattern of social and emotional development: one to two years

During this year, children want to stay near their parents or key carers. They can become very distressed if they cannot see them, even if this is for a few minutes. Interestingly, when they know that their parents are close by, they may then start to explore. This is because in this phase, parents or key carers act as a 'safe base'. The idea of a safe base is that the child knows that someone is there to look out for them and that if they become scared, they can quickly scoot back. If a stranger or a sudden noise occurs, children at this age will want to stay close to their parents.

Babies and toddlers will also start to show some strong emotions towards the end of this year. They may show when they are not pleased by turning their heads or by crying. As they approach two years, they may also have small tantrums when they become frustrated.

In terms of social development, babies and toddlers become more interested in playing during this year. For short periods they may play and explore alone, but they like also to play with an adult or an older sibling.

Social and emotional milestones from one to two years

Age	Social development	Emotional development
15 months	Enjoys playing with adult simple games, e.g. peek-a-boo	Confident to explore environment if parent or key carer is present
18 months	Will bring toys and objects to share and show adults	Shows strong emotions including anger as well as pleasure
2 years	Interested in other children of same age but cannot play with them co-operatively May try to make adults laugh, e.g. put cup on head	Can be determined Tantrums when frustrated May show jealousy if attention given to another child Changes emotions quickly

Read and write

Create a leaflet that explains how children's social and emotional development changes from birth to two years.

Pattern of social and emotional development: two to three years

During this period, children start to become more aware of themselves. This means that they may start to smile or pose when an adult takes a photo of them! Children also start to feel shame when, for example, they have had a toileting accident.

At this age, children's feelings are very strong and they find them very difficult to control. They might hit out at other children, snatch things and also be jealous. They may also have tantrums if they can see something and not have it. As children have limited levels of language and understanding, it is hard to reason with them. If they see something that they want, they will not understand if an adult tells them that it belongs to someone else or that they have to wait until later.

Children also become very interested in other children. They enjoy being near them and you may see **parallel play**. This is when two children are playing with similar toys and in similar ways, but they are not playing together. They are likely to be aware of each other, copy actions and make eye contact.

Jargon buster

Parallel play – where children play alongside each other but not with each other.

Social and emotional milestones from two to three years

Age	Social development	Emotional development
2–3 years	Interesting in being with other children Parallel play is seen Shows concern when others are crying Is not yet sharing or taking turns unless supported by an adult	Knows whether they are a boy or a girl Has quickly changing emotions Likelihood of tantrums when frustrated Has feelings of jealousy and anger towards other children Wants to be close to a parent or a familiar adult Becomes distressed if cannot see parent, family member or key carer

Extend

Find out about the role of the key person in supporting children's emotional development in early years settings. You can find out more by typing the terms 'key person + early years' into a search engine, or visiting these websites:

www.earlyyearscareers.com/eyc/latest-news/the-role-of-the-key-person/

www.earlyyearsmatters.co.uk/eyfs/positive-relationships/key-person-attachment

Pattern of social and emotional development: three to five years

During these two years, children start to show social skills that will allow them to play and enjoy being with other children. This is called **co-operative play**. This development is linked closely to children's language levels.

Most children start to have clear friendships and are able to play co-operatively. Squabbles will occur, but they start to use language to negotiate and explain. By the age of five years, not having a friend to play with can make children feel sad. Interestingly, we will also see that children start to prefer playing with children of the same gender.

Children will also find it easier to cope when their parents are not there, although they will still want to be near familiar adults. While children still have strong emotions at this age, they find it easier to recover if they become upset or are frustrated.

Children are also starting to learn about themselves, based on how others talk and react to them. By five years, children may say that they are 'good' or that they are 'cheeky'.

Jargon buster

Co-operative play – where children can play together and take turns.

Social and emotional milestones from three to five years

Age	Social development	Emotional development
3–5 years	Enjoys playing with other children Can play co-operatively and take turns unless tired Enjoys pretend play and will take on different roles (play becomes more complex from four years)	Will find it easier to separate from parents, especially if they are with familiar adults or with friends Will still show strong emotions but will cope with upsets more easily Can explain their feelings

Check what you know

At what ages would you expect children to show:

- parallel play
- co-operative play?

How understanding the pattern of development is important for early years workers

There are many ways that adults can support children's social and emotional development. The starting point is for adults working with children to know the typical ages and stages of development. This is because adults need to make sure that what they are expecting children to do is fair. A good example of this is playing co-operatively and sharing. Most children under three years old will find it hard to share toys and play co-operatively together. If adults do not know that this is the case, they may be unfair to a child who snatches a toy from another. Adults who know the typical pattern of development will instead help children by playing with them and helping them to take turns.

In the same way, it is important for adults to understand the importance of the bond that children have with their parents. Nature did not intend for young children and their parents to be separated. This means that when young children cannot see their parents, they are likely to cry and become distressed. To help children, all early years settings have a key person system. The idea is that the child develops a bond with one adult in the setting and that this will help them to cope when their parents leave.

Grading

To achieve the assessment criteria 1.1 and also to achieve grading criteria D1, you will need to:

Describe the expected pattern of children's development from birth to five years in the following areas:

- physical development
- language development
- intellectual development
- social and emotional development.

Top marks

In order to get an A grade for the assignment for this unit, you need to show that you can understand the importance of understanding the pattern of children's holistic development.

Can you explain why it is important for early years workers to understand the pattern of children's holistic development from birth to five years?

Try to give examples as well as reasons.

■ Learning Outcome 2: Understand the importance of observations and assessments, and how they support development

Assessment criteria grid

Learning outcomes	Assessment criteria
The learner will:	The learner can:
2 Understand the importance of observations and assessments and how they support development	2.1 Identify different methods to observe children.
	2.2 Describe how observations and assessments can be used to support the development of children.

Have you ever watched a baby drop a rattle and then look down at it? Or have you seen how two-year-olds can be shy with strangers? By watching children, early years workers learn a lot about their stage of development. In this section we will consider how early years settings observe children. We also think about how **observations** and **assessments** are used to support children's development.

Jargon buster

Observations – noticing what children are doing and recording it, usually by writing it down.

Assessment – using observations to work out children's stage of development.

2.1 Identify different methods to observe children

There are many methods that early years workers use to identify children's stage of development. This information is then used to help recognise their stage of development and interests but also to identify when they need additional support.

Information collected by observation

There is some basic information that is always included when early years workers observe children:

- name of child
- date and time of when observation took place
- name of person carrying out the observation.

In addition, other information may be added during or at the start of observations, such as:

- age of the child at the time of the observation, usually in years and months
- purpose of the observation, for example, 'To look at Kyle's play with other children'
- where the child was when the observation was carried out and what the child was doing
- who the child was with when the observation was carried out, for example, other children or adults.

Confidentiality

Early years workers cannot pass on information about children's development or their family to other people unless they have permission to do so. It means that observations and assessments have to be put away in children's records once they are completed. Every early years settings has a policy about confidentiality.

When students are asked to carry out observations for their courses, they have to change children's names or use initials. This stops other people from identifying the child and the family.

Accuracy of information

It is essential that observations and assessments are kept up to date and are accurate. This is because decisions about how best to help a child will be based on them. A child who is assessed as progressing well, but who is not, may not gain the support that is needed. On the other hand, having a child who is assessed as having difficulties may cause parents to become very anxious. When inaccurate assessments are given, there is also a danger that children are given activities and play opportunities that are not suitable for them. This may not help children to make progress, or they may make the children frustrated.

Narrative methods of observation

Narrative methods of observation are written methods. A narrative method will describe what a child is doing or has done, for example, 'Jack is playing with wooden bricks. He is using one brick at a time to build a tower.' Narrative methods can also be called 'free description'. Narrative observations may record what a child is doing over a few seconds or much longer. Sometimes photographs or film clips are used with narrative observations.

Name of child   Jodie B.
Age   3 years 9 months
Observer   Hayley D.
Date of observation   14/9/16
Time   10.08 am

Jodie is playing lego. She is on the floor next to Sam and Freddie. She takes out lego pieces from box, one by one. She is singing to herself. She smiles at Sam and Freddie and then giggles. She says 'I am building the biggest, the very biggest tower in the whole world!' She stands up and says to Freddie 'You have to help me. And you Sam.' The boys ignore her and carry on with their models. Jodie keeps taking out bricks one by one. She starts to put one brick on another. She says aloud 'It's getting bigger!' She adds one more brick and says 'And bigger!' She then counts the number of bricks that she has put together. There are five bricks and she touches each one as she says the number.

She calls across the room to Katie. 'Come and help me.' Katie comes across and Jodie invites her to build a princess tower with her. She asks Katie what colour the tower should be. She shows Katie what she has built. She asks Katie if they should start again. Katie shakes her head. Jodie asks her if she would like to put the next brick on. She holds out two bricks for Katie. 'Which one shall we put now?'

A narrative method of observation

How to carry out a narrative method

All you need is a pen and a piece of paper. Once the basic information has been recorded, the idea is to write down what the child is doing. It can be helpful to decide ahead what to focus on, for example, physical development, language or social skills. This means that it can be easier to decide what to write. Try to be precise as you write. It is good practice not to make any judgements when writing narrative methods, but simply to write down what is happening.

After you have finished

Most people find it hard to write neatly or to keep up with what the child is doing. It can be helpful to re-read what you have written straight away, and if necessary produce a neater or more accurate copy. If you decide to do this, you should make sure that you do not significantly change your wording.

Advantages and disadvantages of narrative methods

Advantages:

- needs no preparation
- can be used to observe all areas of development
- can be used to observe more than one area of development at once.

Disadvantages:

- can be hard to write everything down quickly
- the observer is likely to have to keep stopping, or to choose what to focus on
- can be hard to record accurately and without judgement.

Checklist and tick chart

The checklist and the tick chart are very similar. They are simple ways of assessing children's skills. A list of statements is prepared, for example, 'Is able to put on coat without fastening it up'; 'Is able to use spoon to feed'. The statements are normally based on milestones for children's development or outcomes from the early years curriculum.

The observer puts a tick or writes a note when the child is showing the skill.

Name of child:	Date of assessment:	Observer:	
Physical skill	With support/sometimes	Skill achieved	Comments
Runs and can stop and start easily			
Runs using whole foot			
Walks upstairs and downstairs holding on using two feet to each stair			
Walks into large ball when trying to kick it			
Can move forward on a sit and ride toy			

Carrying out a checklist and tick chart

It is important to read all the statements first and check what they mean. The observer then has to decide whether to ask the child to do the skill. If not, the observer has to keep watching the child and see whether he or she shows the skill while in the session. This can take a lot of time!

When the child has attempted the skill, the observer has to decide whether or not the child can manage the skill on the checklist.

Advantages and disadvantages of checklist and tick charts

Advantages:

- easy to fill in and can be completed fairly quickly
- can be repeated to see if a child has made progress
- keeps the observer focused on specific skills.

Disadvantages:

- observers may come to different conclusions about whether a child has mastered a skill, for example, a child might be able to do it with encouragement
- does not show how quickly or confidently a child managed a task or skill.

Children are also likely to act differently when they know the observer. They may try harder to please the adult and make an extra effort. A good example of this is when children are sitting around a table. They may offer to share food with other children because an adult is there. This means that when children know that they are being watched, the results of the observation might be different. In some situations, children may actually not do as well as they may become nervous.

- Can you think of a situation when you were being observed by someone?
- How did it change what you did or what you felt?

Event sample

An event sample is not strictly an observation – it is a record of events. Early years settings are most likely to use event samples to look at children's behaviour; for example, if a child often bites, an event sample would be used to work out when and why the child bites. It is possible, though, to use event samples to understand an individual's language and social development.

After a few 'events' have been recorded, the early years worker can then see if there are any patterns to the behaviours being shown. It might be that a child only bites in the morning just after break or a child only cries at meal times. Understanding patterns can then help early years workers to think about how best to support the child.

Time period: w/c 6th Feb

Name of child: Karl

Age: 4 years 1 month

Key person: Jayne

Event to be recorded: Tantrum

Time and date	Context	What happened	What happened afterwards
6/2/17 10.12am	Cloakroom • other children in cloakroom 1 adult supervising	Karl wanted to hold Amy's hat. Amy would not let him. Karl snatched hat. Adult gave it back to Amy. Tantrum started.	Took five minutes to calm down. Key person stayed near. Reassured Karl after tantrum finished.
6/2/17 10.48am	Snack table 1 adult interacting 2 other children	Karl wanted to help himself to the fruit plate. It was not his turn. The adult reminded him to wait. Tantrum started immediately.	Tantrum lasted 7 minutes. Key person came over. Stayed near Karl and reassured him afterwards. Karl ate his snack quickly and asked for more.
6/2/17 11.30am	Tidying up in construction area 1 adult supporting 3 children to tidy away	Karl ignored the request to start tidying away. He carried on playing. Another children started to take some of the bricks away from him. Tantrum began.	Tantrum lasted 4 minutes. Key person came over and stayed near Karl. Afterward Karl pointed to the bricks and said 'mine'.

An event sample

How an event sample works

A prepared sheet is drawn up which will be used to record the behaviour or 'event'. The early years setting might want to know why a child often pinches other children, or in which circumstances a child is more likely to talk.

When the 'event' happens, the early years worker will then fill in the sheet. They record the time, what happened, who the child was with and any reasons why the event happened. Some event samples also have a space to write down what happened next.

After a few events, the early years worker will then look back to see if there are any patterns to the child's behaviour. If the early years setting has tried to help the child, the event sample can also be used to help check that the strategy they are using is working.

Advantages and disadvantages of an event sample

Advantages:

- it is possible to pick up patterns or triggers for behaviours
- can be used to check that strategies are working.

Disadvantages:

- adults may not always be there to see what has caused the 'event'
- adults may forget to fill in the sheet promptly.

Theory in action

Mel is four years old. She often has tantrums. The early years setting have decided to carry out an event sample. Every time Mel has a tantrum, the team write down when it happened, where it happened and also why it happened. Mel's parents have been asked to do this at home.

After a week, the event sample shows that Mel has had 14 tantrums. A pattern emerges that it is often when Mel is very tired – before nap time and also before bedtime. The early years setting and the parents agree that bed and nap time should be earlier. The next week, Mel only has two tantrums. The conclusion is that Mel was getting overtired.

- What was the event that was being recorded?
- Why was it important that the time of day was written down?
- How was the event sample used to support Mel's behaviour?

Time sample

A time sample is used to see what a child is doing over an hour or over a session. The information can help a setting to see what activities a child enjoys, where the child goes and who the child likes to play with.

Name of child: Jasmine			
Age: 3 years 2 months			
Focus for observation: Play preferences			
Name of observer: Key person			
Time	Location	Present	Observation
9.15	Indoors sand tray	Bryony	Jasmine is filling a small bucket with sand using a spoon. Bryony is holding the small bucket.
9.25	Indoors sand tray	Bryony	Jasmine and Bryony are decorating a sandcastle with buttons and lids. Jasmine says 'We don't want any more of these [lids] do we?'
9.35	Indoors sand tray	Bryony Sam	Jasmine says to Sam 'You are not allowed to touch our sandcastle.' Her voice is loud and she is pointing at him.
9.45	Sam	Sam	Jasmine is holding a bucket out for Sam. 'You need to fill this!' Sam shakes his head. Jasmine says, 'You have to!'
9.55	Bryony Adult	Bryony Adult	Jasmine and Bryony sit together. Bryony asks Jasmine, 'Do you like banana best?' Jasmine nods her head and opens her mouth. It is full of banana.
10.05	Bryony Alex	Bryony Alex	Jasmine is clearing her plate away. She turns to Alex and says, 'We're going now. But you can play with us when you've finished.' She looks at Bryony and says, 'Baby baby banana.' They both giggle.

A time sample sheet

Activity

Look at the time sample. In pairs consider the following:

- Talk about Jasmine's social and language development.
- What conclusions have you made?

Carrying out a time sample

You need to think about what you would like to observe. You also have to decide on how long you will observe and what the intervals between each observation will be, for example, every ten minutes. A sheet then has to be prepared showing the timings. Once you start observing, you write down what the child is doing for a few seconds. When the next time slot comes, you need to record again.

Advantages and disadvantages of a time sample

Advantages:

- shows what children are doing over a longer period than a narrative record
- can be used to look at different aspects of a child's development.

Disadvantages:

- the observer has to keep an eye on the time
- an interesting event or incident might be missed because it is not in the 'time slot'
- the observer has to be organised and prepare a sheet.

Sociogram

A sociogram is a way of finding out about children's friendship preferences. It is best used on older children.

Carrying out a sociogram

To carry out a sociogram, you need to ask each child about who they like to play with when they are in the setting. It is important that children are asked when they are alone, as otherwise they may be influenced by other children. A note is made of each child's preferences. Afterwards a chart is created which needs to be analysed to see if any children are frequently named by other children, or if there are any children who are not named by others.

Children who are named as being friends			Anna					
	Anna		Gracie		Tom	Josie	Josie	Gracie
	Gracie	Adam	Tom	Gracie	Ahmed	Sarah	Gracie	Josie
	Adam	Sarah	Adam	Sarah	Sarah	Anna	Tom	Ahmed
Name of child being asked about friendships	Sarah	Lee	Ahmed	Josie	Adam	Gracie	Anna	Tom

A sociogram

Activity

Look carefully at the sociogram chart.

- Which child has not been named by the other children?
- Which child has been frequently named by the other children?

Advantages and disadvantages of sociograms

Advantages:

- can be useful as a starting point to find out more about children's friendships and who they play with, although further observations would need to be done
- useful with older children who may be playing out of sight of adults.

Disadvantages:

- can be very unreliable. Children might not name a child who is absent, and might name children who they do not play with but whom they admire
- can only be used with older children who are likely to be more settled in their friendships.

Using technology for observations

Technology has been increasingly used to observe children. Early years settings routinely use cameras to film and take photographs of children. Some early years settings use software that directly link the observations to children's electronic records. In addition, parents can send in recordings or look at their children's file online.

Sharing observations with colleagues

Once observations are made, then the information gained has to be considered. If you observe a child doing something of interest, it is good practice to share this information with the child's key person as soon as possible, even if you have not written it down. The key person is the person who helps the child feel safe and secure, but who also observes and plans for the child's development. The child's key person will also be responsible for gaining and sharing information with the child's parents. As we saw earlier, it is essential that when observations are accurate when they are shared.

2.2 Describe how observations and assessments can be used to support the development of children

Observations and assessments of children are used by early years settings in a variety of ways to support the development of children. In this section we look at the main ways in which they are used by early years settings.

Five things to know about observations and assessments

Make sure that you know:
1) The importance of observations and assessments being accurate.
2) How observations and assessments are used to check the pattern of children's development.
3) Why observations and assessments are shared with parents and professionals.
4) How observations and assessments are used to plan play and activities for children.
5) How observations and assessments are used to understand children's behaviour.

Checking the pattern of children's development

It is important for early years workers to know whether children are developing typically. Some observations and assessments will focus on this. By checking children's development, we can see whether or not children are making typical progress.

There are many reasons why children may not be showing typical development. In some cases there might be a medical condition, or the child has a learning difficulty. When children's progress is not typical, the early years worker will need to discuss options with parents. In some cases, the child might need additional adult time or specific play opportunities. In some cases the child will need to be referred to another professional for an assessment (see page 100, for more detail and providing information for professionals).

Theory in action

Vivek is four years old. He is due to start school in September. He likes playing with trains and other toys, but mostly by himself. He can become very frustrated when other children join him. He has settled into the nursery well, and is very happy if he can play alone. He often talks to himself. His early years worker has carried out an observation. The assessment suggests that while some aspects of his development are good, his social skills are not typical.

- Look back at page 86 on social and emotional development. At what age are most children enjoying playing with others?
- Is Vivek's social development typical?
- Why is it important that the early years worker has noticed his development?

Extend

In England, it is a legal requirement for all early years settings working with two-year-old children to carry out an assessment. This is known as the two-year-old check. The information has to be shared with parents and any concerns about a child's development have to be discussed.

Find out more about ...

... the two-year-old check by typing 'EYFS two year old check' into a search engine. Use the information you gain to create a handout for other learners.

Planning to support development and children's interests

It is much easier to plan play and activities for children when their stage of development is known. Early years settings use the information gained from observations and assessments to plan activities that support the next steps of a child's development. Some observations are also carried out to look at what children enjoy doing. This allows the early years worker to plan activities that are based on the child's interests.

Understanding children's behaviour

Some observations and assessments help early years workers to understand why a child is showing unwanted behaviour. By understanding why a child is behaving in a certain way, it is possible to plan routines and activities to support the child. In some cases, the child might need more adult time, or perhaps the child is very tired on some days and needs less demanding activities.

Sharing information with parents

Early years settings regularly share information about children's development with parents. This is important because parents often want to find out more about how their child is doing and also what they are interested in. Parents often share information about their child's development and interests at home too. This information is used by early years workers to help plan activities in the setting.

Theory in action

Josh is two years old. He is at nursery five mornings a week. His early years worker is talking to his parent about his progress in language. She tells the parent that Josh is starting to use a lot of words now and that his language is typical for his age. She mentions that he seems interested in zoo animals and has a favourite book about them. His parent says that at home he also loves looking at books with pictures of dogs in them.

- What has the parent said that might help the early years worker plan for Josh's interests?
- Give an example of how the early years worker could use this information.

Providing information to professionals

Early years settings will also share information about children to other professionals. This is important when children go to another setting or move to school. It allows the new early years worker to understand what the child can do and any areas of development that need to be further supported.

Sometimes information might be shared with other professionals. This might include speech and language therapists, physiotherapists or health visitors. Information is usually shared with these professionals because they are working with the child and the family. This might be because the child has a developmental need. Remember that we can only comment on the child's development when they are with us. This is because children may show different behaviours at the setting, or might be able to do different things when they are at home or with other people. As we have already seen, it is also important that information is up to date and accurate.

Where there are concerns about a child's welfare, information may also be shared with social workers. If there are no concerns, early years settings cannot pass on information about a child without the parents' consent.

My life as a speech and language assistant

I trained as a nursery nurse but then became a speech and language assistant. I love my job. I work alongside a speech and language therapist. One of the aspects of my role is to work directly with children and often their parents. I show parents how to put into practice the suggestions that the speech and language therapist has made. I also observe children and record their progress so that I can discuss it with the therapist. This is one aspect of the role that I really enjoy as we are often able to see that children have made good progress.

Learning to observe children and track their progress is a real skill, but it is fascinating. I also love trying to think up new activities that will be fun for children, but will also help them make progress.

■ Learning Outcome 3: Understand factors that may affect children's holistic development

Learning outcomes	Assessment criteria
The learner will:	The learner can:
3 Understand factors that may affect children's holistic development.	3.1 Explain factors that may affect children's holistic development.

Have you ever wondered why we are all so different? Why every child has their own personality and ways of responding? In this section we look at some of the factors that affect the way children grow and develop.

High priority

Make sure that you know what the term 'holistic development' means.

3.1 Factors that may affect children's holistic development

There are many factors that can affect children's holistic development. In this section we are going to separate them into **personal factors** and **external factors**:

- **Personal factors** are about your inherited traits and also what happened to you before and immediately after you were born.
- **External factors** are about where and how you grew up. They also include the events and experiences that you have had.

Personal factors

The table below shows some of the personal factors that can affect children's development. It is hard to know exactly how any personal factor will affect a child.

Personal factors that can affect development

Personal factor	Example	How it might affect development
Physical traits Some physical traits are linked to genetic inheritance	Height, physical strength, face shape, eye colour	Adults often give taller children more responsibility and so more opportunities. Children who are not happy with the way they look might not feel as confident.
Medical conditions Some medical conditions are more likely as a result of genetic inheritance	Diabetes, asthma, sickle cell anaemia	Feeling poorly might stop children from joining in activities. They might feel different from other children. Children might fall behind with their schoolwork if they need time off school.
Learning difficulties Some learning difficulties are more likely as a result of genetic inheritance	Autistic spectrum conditions, dyslexia	Children may need more support to master some skills. Some children with social learning difficulties may find it harder to make friends.
Disabilities Some disabilities are linked to genetic inheritance, while others may occur during pregnancy and birth	Deafness, sight problems, cerebral palsy, spina bifida	Children with a disability might need additional support or equipment to join in activities. They might feel different to other children.
Personality and temperament	Shyness, curiosity, outgoing	Children who are more outgoing might be more interested in making friends. This will help their social development. Children who are curious are more likely to try out new experiences and explore more. This will support their intellectual development.
Pregnancy and birth How healthy a mother is during pregnancy can affect a child's later development	German measles, fetal alcohol syndrome, spina bifida, developmental difficulties	Problems during pregnancy and birth can cause medical conditions and disabilities. This can affect how easily children learn and grow.

Theory in action

Lee is five years old. He has asthma and often has time off school because of chest infections. He is a quiet boy who finds it hard to ask questions and to talk to teachers. He also finds it hard to make friends, and because of his asthma he cannot always join in when the other children are playing physical games. His mother is worried that because of the time off school and also his personality, he might be falling behind with his reading and maths.

- Identify the personal factors involved in Lee's development.
- Explain how each of the personal factors might affect Lee's development.
- Why is it important for the adults working with Lee to recognise these personal factors?

Extend

A healthy pregnancy can help children's later development. Choose one of the following areas to research more

- smoking and pregnancy
- alcohol and pregnancy
- folic acid and pregnancy.

Create a leaflet that gives advice to pregnant women.

External factors

External factors are the experiences, events and relationships that affect children's development. For children the list of external factors is very long. The chart shows some of the key factors that contribute to children's development.

External factors that can affect development

External factor	Example	How it might affect development
Love and interaction Children thrive if they feel loved and have plenty of positive attention from the adults who care for them	Cuddles, time to talk, being spoken to positively, being listened to	Children learn to talk and communicate with others. They learn how to behave nicely towards others.
Stimulation and play Children benefit if there are opportunities to play, talk and do different things	Going to different places, doing different things, playing with adults and other children, sharing books	Children who are being stimulated are likely to learn to talk quickly. They will also have opportunities to try out different things and develop a range of skills, e.g. co-ordination, social skills.
Physical conditions Children need shelter, warmth and to be physically safe. They also need room to move and explore	Warm home, opportunities to go outdoors, space to play indoors	Children who are in safe and healthy physical conditions are less likely to have accidents and become ill. If there is plenty of room to move and explore, they are more likely to develop physical skills.
Food and drink Children need food and drink that is nutritious and healthy. This helps them to grow and have the energy to explore, move and learn.	Developing good food habits including enjoying vegetables and foods high in nutrients	Children who have a healthy diet are less likely to become ill. They are likely to be able to move easily if they are the correct weight for their height.

Jargon buster

Interaction – communication that is two-way and enjoyable.

These children are four years years old and are playing in a pre-school

Factors that might negatively affect development

We have seen some of the key factors that might help children's development. But life is not always perfect. Some children will also experience events that may affect negatively their development.

Family breakdown and bereavement

Being loved and valued is important for children. When families break down or if someone dies, it can affect children's emotional and social development. They may not know how to cope.

Parenting problems

Being a parent is not easy – it is very hard work. If a parent is not coping because of depression, illness or taking drugs, they might not meet children's basic needs. This can mean that children do not get the love and attention they need, or the physical care.

Activity

Having read about poverty and young children, go back to table on personal factors affecting development on page 102. Which personal factors are linked to poverty?

Poverty

When families do not have enough money, parents might find it hard to provide everything children need. They might not have anywhere safe or healthy to live. Families might not eat a healthy diet or there might be few toys and days out.

Accident or illness

A life-changing accident or illness might affect children's development. They might not be able to go out and play with other children, and this could affect their social development. They might miss out on experiences and stimulation, and this could affect their learning.

Extend

Find out more about how accidents can be prevented. Visit this website and take two of their quizzes: www.capt.org.uk/get-involved/quizzes.

Discrimination and bullying

In Unit 1 we looked at the importance of inclusion. Children who are discriminated against or are bullied by others are likely to lose confidence. They may not want to try out new things and this can prevent new learning. Bullying and discrimination can also affect how they make relationships with other children.

Check what you know

Can you think of five things that might contribute to or negatively affect a child's holistic development?

Explain how it might affect development.

Combining personal and external factors

We have split up personal and external factors, but they often work together. A good example of this is personality. It is thought that personality is partly genetic (personal), but what happens to the child (external) is also important.

Theory in action

Using these examples, explain how personal and external factors are linked together.

- Max was always a little shy and unsure of meeting new people. After being given a role in the school play, he has really grown in confidence.
- Andrew was born premature and underweight. The doctors said that he was likely to have some learning difficulties. His parents have played and talked to him. He does have learning difficulties, but these are mild.

Identical twins, Alice and Dora

Activity

Look at the photograph of Alice and Dora. They look the same because they have exactly the same genes. Alice loves looking at books and talking to adults. Dora prefers to play outdoors building dens by herself.

● Do you think that their development will be exactly the same?
● What strengths might each child have?

Five things to know about factors affecting development

1) Holistic development is children's development considered as a whole.
2) Children's development can be affected by personal and external factors.
3) Personal factors are linked to genetic make-up, pregnancy and birth.
4) External factors are about the experiences and environment a child grows up in.
5) Personal factors and external factors can work together to influence development.

Grading

To achieve the assessment criteria D4, you should:

Describe the factors which can affect the holistic development of children.

■ Learning Outcome 4: Understand how to use everyday care, routines and activities to support independence, health, safety and well-being

Assessment criteria grid

Learning outcomes	Assessment criteria
The learner will:	The learner can:
4 Understand how to use everyday care routines and activities to support independence, health, safety and well-being.	4.1 Describe everyday activities which promote independence.
	4.2 Explain how daily routines and activities can meet care needs and support the well-being of children.

We have seen that children's development changes over time. In order to grow and develop, children's needs have to be met. In this section we look at the benefits of care routines and activities for children.

High priority

Make sure that you have learnt a range of everyday activities that will support children's development.

Look carefully at children's care needs at different ages and stages of development.

4.1 Describe everyday activities which promote independence

One of the most important things that adults help children to do over time is to become independent. This is important as when children can do things for themselves, they grow in confidence. Let's start by looking at children's basic needs:

- sleep and rest
- physical activity
- a balanced diet including water
- suitable clothing for the weather
- personal hygiene, for example, washing skin, care of hair and teeth
- safe environment.

Activity

Look at the list of children's basic needs. Talk to a partner about whether or not they are different to your basic needs.

Can you remember how old you were before you could get ready for bed, take a bath or shower, and clean your own teeth?

Every basic need is important for children. Adults have to ensure that all of children's needs are met and in ways that are appropriate for children's ages.

Sleep and rest

All humans need to sleep and rest. Babies and young children need to sleep a lot more than adults. This is because they are growing and also learning new skills. During sleep the body produces a growth hormone. It also produces other hormones that keep the body healthy.

Sleep is important for children's overall health. During sleep, the body is able to repair cells and fight infections. Overtired children also find it hard to cope with the demands of a busy day. They may not concentrate and listen, and might find it hard to manage their feelings and behaviour.

Five things to know about sleep and rest

1) Sleep and rest are important for children's growth and development.
2) They prevent children from becoming ill.
3) Overtired children find it hard to manage their emotions and behaviour.
4) During sleep, the brain stores and processes information.
5) Sleep is easier to manage as part of a routine.

Physical activity

Every day children need to be physically active. This might be walking to the shops or to school. Playing outdoors is a great way for children to be physical active.

There are many health and well-being benefits to physical activity. Children who are active are likely to have stronger hearts, bones and muscles. Physical activity also helps children to feel good and confident as they master skills. Physical activity, especially outdoors, also helps children to build a healthy appetite, helps their digestion and also helps them to sleep better.

Balanced diet including water

Young children need food and water in order to grow and survive. It is important though that they have the food in the right quantities for their age and stage of development. The term 'balanced diet' is used when children are getting meals and snacks that meet their needs for growth but in the right quantities.

As well as food children also need to drink. Water is the best drink to give children, although babies and toddlers need milk.

When children have a balanced diet, they have enough energy to move and to play. A balanced diet is also needed for children to fight off infection and for growth.

When children do not have a **balanced diet**, they can become overweight which can affect their health and also their confidence. Interestingly, a balanced diet for children of all ages has very little or no sugar in it. This means that foods that have high levels of sugar in them should not be offered to children. High levels of sugar in children's diet can cause children's teeth to decay and also can cause them to become overweight.

Five things to know about a balanced diet and water

1) A balanced diet provides energy.
2) It helps children to grow in line with their age and stage of development.
3) It provides children with the vitamins and minerals needed for healthy teeth, bones and gums.
4) It is important for preventing illness.
5) A balanced diet does not include sugary foods.

Extend

Find out more about the portion sizes and food needs of young children. Visit this website and download 'A practical guide to eating well': www.cwt.org.uk.

Suitable clothing and footwear for weather

Children need clean clothing and footwear that is right for the weather. Clothing is important to keep children warm in winter and in summer to protect the skin from the sun. Suitable clothing for children keeps them comfortable and allows them to play easily.

Suitable footwear allows children to walk and run safely. It is important for footwear to fit children well as the bones in the feet are still developing. If shoes are too tight or too big, children's feet can be damaged. Babies are not normally put in shoes until they are walking, and instead wear socks or other soft covering to keep their feet warm.

Children need clean clothes, especially underwear and nightwear. If clothes are dirty, children may pick up infections. Babies and toddlers often need several changes of clothes because they wear nappies and may be messy eaters!

Five things to know about suitable clothing and footwear

1) Suitable clothes and footwear allow children to move easily and play.
2) Shoes and footwear must be the right size.
3) Clothes must be kept clean to prevent the skin from becoming infected.
4) In the summer, children need clothes (including hats) that will protect them from sunburn.
5) Clothes in winter protect the skin from the wind and keep children warm.

Explain why these children are appropriately dressed for rainy weather

Weather	Footwear	Clothing
Summer, sunshine		Sun hat Sunglasses
Winter Cold weather	Boots or warm shoes	

Activity

Can you complete this table, giving examples of children's clothing for different seasons?

Personal hygiene

Personal hygiene means keeping the skin, hair and teeth clean. Babies and young children's immune systems are still developing. This means that they find it hard to fight infections. To prevent the most common infections, adults have to make sure that children's skin, hair and teeth are kept clean. Children are likely to need to bath or shower every day. In addition, babies and toddlers wearing nappies need to have the skin around the nappy area cleaned every time they have a nappy change.

Children's hands need washing several times a day. They need to wash their hands before eating, after being outdoors and also after going to the toilet. Washing hands is one of the most important ways of preventing infections.

As part of caring for the skin, there may also be times when sun cream will need to be applied. Sun cream is needed to prevent the skin from becoming burnt and also to prevent skin cancers later in life. It is important to follow the latest guidelines.

Activity

Find out about latest advice to protect children's skin in the sun. Visit www.nhs.uk/Conditions/pregnancy-and-baby/Pages/safety-in-the-sun.aspx:

- What is the current advice for children being outdoors in the sun?
- When should sun cream be applied?

As well as cleaning the skin, children's teeth have to be cleaned twice a day. This prevents **dental decay**.

Children's hair has to be kept clean and brushed. Adults looking after children should watch out for **head lice**, which live on hair. Children can easily pick them up from each other when they are in early years setting.

Jargon buster

Personal hygiene – keeping skin, hair and teeth clean.
Head lice – small insects that lay eggs and live in hair.
Dental decay – destruction of tooth enamel caused by bacteria.

Five things to know about personal hygiene

1) Personal hygiene is important to prevent infection.
2) It keeps children feeling comfortable.
3) It prevents teeth from decaying.
4) Teeth should be cleaned twice a day.
5) Hands should be washed before eating, after going to the toilet and after being outdoors.

Read and write

Around a quarter of children starting school have tooth decay. Find out about how to prevent dental decay by visiting: www.nhs.uk/Livewell/dentalhealth/Pages/Goodhabitskids.aspx

Create a leaflet that helps parents understand more about preventing dental decay.

Extend

Head lice are common in young children. Find out more about their life cycle and how to prevent them. Visit this website: www.nhs.uk/Conditions/Head-lice/Pages/Introduction.aspx

Create a poster that will help other learners understand how to avoid head lice.

Safe and stimulating environment

In Unit 1, we saw that one of the roles of the adult is to provide a safe environment. This is important to prevent accidents. Very young children do not know what is dangerous, and they are often very impulsive. This means that they do or touch things without thinking first. A safe environment means that children can play and explore without risk of a serious injury. Over time children learn how to stay safe indoors and outdoors, but at first it is the job of adults to supervise them and use safety equipment.

If children are not kept safe and have accidents, their development can be affected. This is because the injury itself may be life-changing; for example, a head injury or because they have to take time off school or nursery. This in turn can mean that they fall behind with their learning.

Children also need a stimulating environment where they can see and do new things. Adults need to plan activities, resources and toys to make sure that children can learn from what is available. To do this, they need to think about children's age and stage of development.

Five things to know about a safe and stimulating environment

1) A stimulating environment is important for children's holistic development.
2) A safe and stimulating environment reflects the age and stage of the children's development.
3) A safe environment prevents children from becoming injured.
4) As children develop, they need to learn to assess risks in the environment.
5) Children also need to learn to maintain the environment so that it stays safe and stimulating.

Check what you know

Explain with examples why it is important to prevent accidents and keep children safe.

How to safeguard children to keep them safe and healthy

Independence and self-care skills

We have seen that children's basic needs must be met for them to be healthy and comfortable. One of the roles of the early years worker is to help children learn the skills they need to be able to meet their own needs. These skills are sometimes called 'self-care' skills.

Learning some self-care skills is important for children's holistic development. Here are three ways in which self-care skills can help children's development:

1 Self-care skills help children to gain confidence.
2 They build children's physical skills, especially hand–eye co-ordination.
3 They help children to learn about health and well-being.

The table on page 116 shows the types of self-care skills that children need to learn. Note that some skills will not be fully mastered until children are much older.

Jargon buster

Self-settle – being able to fall asleep alone without being rocked, rubbed or held by an adult.

Basic need	Self-care skill
Sleep and rest	Be able to recognise when tired
	Be able to **self-settle**
Physical activity	Be able to enjoy playing outdoors
	Be able to manage risks
	Be able to use different equipment and show different skills
A balanced diet including water	Learn to feed themselves and serve food
	Develop a taste for a wide range of healthy foods, especially fruit and vegetables
	Learn the social skills of meal times
Suitable clothing for the weather	Learn how to put on and take off clothes and footwear
	Learn to choose clothes and footwear appropriate for the weather
Personal hygiene	Learn when and how to wash hands
	Develop the skills to go to the toilet without support
	Understand the importance of cleaning teeth
	Enjoy bath/shower time and be able to wash themselves
	Be able to brush or comb hair
Safe and stimulating environment	Learn how to tidy away things that might cause an accident
	Learn how to tidy toys away so that other children can enjoy using them
	Recognise what might be dangerous
	Learn how to move safely around the environment, e.g. not running indoors

Check what you know

Give an example of a self-care skill that will help prevent infection.

How everyday activities can support children's independence

We have seen that children will over time need to become independent. Let's look at some of the ways in which adults can help children through everyday activities.

Sleep and rest

Routines are helpful in helping children to sleep and rest. Most children need a period of winding down and relaxation first. This might include quiet activities such as sharing a book with an early years worker.

Children can be helped to become more independent with their sleep and rest if they are involved in getting ready. Children aged between three and five years can be encouraged to put on their nightwear, while toddlers can choose a story before nap or bedtime. It is also important for adults to encourage children to recognise when they are feeling tired.

Read and write

Create a leaflet with tips about how to help children sleep and rest. You can carry out more research by visiting: www.nhs.uk/Livewell/Childrenssleep/Pages/childrenssleephome.aspx.

Physical activity

Children can be helped to become independent in physical activity if early years workers encourage them to try out new skills, and provide them with equipment and activities that are challenging but manageable. For a toddler, this might be using a large soft ball rather than a small bouncy one, or a tricycle which does not have pedals. As children become older, early years workers need to help children learn to manage risks. They could ask children to think about possible dangers when climbing and then encourage children to think about how they can reduce the risk.

Balanced diet

There are many activities around meal and snack times that can encourage children to develop independence.

Feeding

When babies show an interest in spoons, they should be given one so that they can start to feed themselves. From around nine months, babies can be given some foods that they can manage by themselves. This might be pieces of soft fruit or bread. These type of foods are known as **finger foods** as babies can use their fingers to eat them. Babies and toddlers can also be encouraged to drink, firstly from beakers with lids and then open cups over time.

The role of the adult is to judge when children might be ready to start learning a new skill, and then to encourage and praise children. At first all children are messy, but with time and with practice, they become more skilful. Once children have mastered using a spoon, they should be encouraged to try out other cutlery.

After eating, children should also be involved in wiping and drying their faces and washing their hands.

Jargon buster

Finger foods – foods that babies can eat without adult help.

Preparation

Children can also be involved in the preparation of meals and snacks. As soon as children start to walk, they can help take things to the table. Older children can lay the table and also afterwards help to clear away. From around two years, with support, children can also pour their own drinks and start to serve themselves. Older children can help with simple tasks in preparing snacks and food such as washing fruit.

> ## Check what you know
>
> Make a list of three ways that mealtimes help children's development.

Suitable clothing and footwear for weather

Getting dressed and undressed is a frequent activity for babies and young children. Adults can encourage them to become involved from an early age. Interestingly, most children learn to take things off before they can put them on. This means that with a baby from around nine months, an adult can partly pull a sock and then the baby can finish off. Similarly, if adults undo buttons and zips, toddlers can often take off shoes, coats and jackets.

As children can be slow to dress, it is important that adults give them plenty of time. By encouraging children to do as much as they can, they can become increasingly independent. This means that most children are able to dress and undress at four years old, apart from zips and laces.

Children also need adults to help them learn about appropriate clothing. Adults may do this by commenting on the weather and then talking about what will be needed. As children get older, adults can then ask children what they think they will need to wear.

Adults can also help children by encouraging them to think about the type of activity they will be doing. Many early years settings encourage children to put on aprons, for example, for messy activities such as painting or playing in water. Over time, children start to remember for themselves that they will need an apron.

What physical skills is this child practising by putting on their own shoes?

Personal hygiene

Children need to gradually learn how to manage their personal hygiene. This takes time and there are many aspects to personal hygiene. Adults working with children also need to talk to children's parents about how best to care for skin, hair and teeth.

Skin

Children need to learn to keep themselves clean. Most babies and young children need a shower or bath once a day. In addition, they will also need their faces and hands washing at different times of the day.

To help children learn the skills so that they become independent, it is important that adults make the process enjoyable. At bath or shower time, this might mean allowing babies and young children to play with the water for some time. It may also mean playing a game when face washing. When children are ready, the adult can encourage the child to become involved in the process. At shower or bathtime, this could mean getting the towels ready, or when washing hands after going to the toilet, squeezing the soap dispenser.

When it comes to washing hands, children can also learn from copying an adult. If a child sees an adult washing and drying their hands properly, they are more likely to do it. Adults also need to praise children when they have a go.

Hair

Children's hair will need to be brushed, combed and in some cases styled. It is important to make this fun for children and to be gentle with their hair. Children often prefer to sit in front of a mirror so that they can see what is happening. Once children take an interest, it is important to encourage them to help. This might mean a toddler wanting to hold the brush or an older child having a go. As children get older, you can also make brushing hair a game so that children pretend to be at a hairdresser's.

Many young children dislike having their hair washed. Early years workers can help children to be independent by letting children put a small amount of shampoo on their hair and encouraging them to rub it in. Older children might be able to rinse some of their hair, but they will need help in getting it fully rinsed. Singing songs while washing hair can help to reassure children and also act as a distraction.

Why is it important for children to have their hair combed or brushed?

Teeth

Most dentists say that children will not be able to properly clean their teeth until they are at least eight years old. Children can help though, by putting toothpaste on the brush and also starting the process of brushing. It is important that adults finish off the brushing process so that every tooth has been cleaned.

Safe and stimulating environment

We have seen that children need to be in a safe and stimulating environment as this supports their holistic development. One of the activities that children can help with is tidying up. Keeping areas tidy can prevent accidents, especially falls. It also keeps areas stimulating as toys and resources can be easier to find and remain attractive. Most early years settings encourage children to put things away and might build time into the session for tidying up. Toddlers can help by bringing things over to an adult, while older children can take responsibility for small areas.

As children develop, they can also be encouraged to think about how to stay safe. This might mean reminding them to walk rather than run indoors.

Why is it important for children to learn to tidy up?

Fair expectations

In order to help children become independent, adults need to have fair expectations of them. This is one of the reasons why early years workers need to know about patterns of children's development. If an adult asks a child to do something that is too hard, the child will become frustrated. They may also stop trying and this could have short- or even long-term effects on holistic development.

Theory in action

Russell is working for the first time in a nursery. He is asked to supervise the two-year-old children at lunch time. He puts out knives and forks for the children. One of the children starts to use their fingers to eat. Russell tells the child off. Another child puts the knife in their mouth.

- Why should Russell have found about typical patterns of development?
- What should Russell have provided for this age group?
- What are the potential dangers of not knowing about children's patterns of development?

My life as a manager

I work as a manager of a large day nursery. I have been working with children for nearly 25 years. We have over 80 children here. Nearly all of our children are here for 10 hours a day. This means that we serve breakfast, lunch and a tea. We are responsible for many of the care needs of children such as cleaning teeth, naps and toileting.

When I first started my career, the focus was just on completing these tasks as quickly as possible, but now we encourage children to be involved. Even the babies are given a face wipe after meals so that they can start to clean their own faces. We also use care activities as learning opportunities. We talk to children about why they need to clean their teeth and hands, or ask them what they need to wear outdoors. As part of my role, parents often ask me for their advice. The most common questions relate to sleep and food!

4.2 Explain how daily routines and activities can meet care needs and support the well-being of children

We have seen how the basic needs of children need to be met each day. We have also seen ways in which children can start to become independent. In this section we will look at the importance of routines, and also how some of the everyday activities that we have looked at earlier can promote children's holistic development.

LEARNING OUTCOME 4: UNDERSTAND HOW TO USE EVERYDAY CARE, ROUTINES & ACTIVITIES TO SUPPORT INDEPENDENCE, HEALTH, SAFETY & WELL-BEING

121

The importance of routines

Every early years setting has a routine. Routines are everyday events that meet children's basic needs. A good example of this is mealtimes. Children need to be fed and so mealtimes will always be part of the routine. A good routine will therefore meet children's care needs.

Routines will also help children to feel secure. This is because they know what will be happening at different times. This is very important for young children, especially when they are not with their parents.

It is good practice in early years settings to talk to parents about their children's needs. This is very important when caring for babies and toddlers, as they will all have their own routine for feeding and sleeping.

Practical ways in which routines meet children's needs

It can be useful to look at ways in which routines meet children's holistic needs and development. Here is a routine for a pre-school setting:

9.00 am arrival Each child is met by their key person before going off to explore the toys and resources that have been put out.

- Children's emotional needs are being met because they are greeted by their key person.
- Children's intellectual needs are being met because they can explore and play.

9.45 am Outdoor area is opened once staff have checked it. Children invited to tidy up if they want to go outdoors. They are also reminded to collect their coats and wellingtons if the weather is wet.

- Children's physical development needs are being met because they can play outdoors.
- Children's needs to keep warm and safe are being met because they are helped to dress suitably for the weather.

10.30–11.00 am Snack area is available for children. All children are reminded to wash their hands before eating. Children are encouraged to sit and talk with their friends and/or key person

- Children's needs for food and water are being met.
- Infections are being prevented because children are encouraged to wash their hands.
- Children's social development is being supported because children are encouraged to sit and talk.
- Children's emotional development is being supported because children can sit with their key person.

10.30–11 am Story area available. An opportunity for children to share a book while sitting and resting.

- Children's need for rest is met.
- Language development is supported.

11.40 am Children indoors and outdoors are encouraged to help tidy away toys and resources alongside adults.

- Children learn about tidying up. The environment is kept safe.
- Children's social and emotional development is supported as they join in tidying up and also feel successful.

11.50 am Children encouraged to collect their coats and get dressed ready to go home.

- Children develop physical skills as they get dressed.

12.00 pm Home time

Activity

Look at the following afternoon routine in a toddler room. Timings are approximate and will depend on children's interests, care needs and also the weather.

1.00 pm Toddlers who need to nap are put down to sleep. Nappies are checked and changed where necessary, before and after naps. The area where they sleep is checked to make sure it is clean and safe.

Toddlers who are not sleeping share time with their key person, looking at books or playing simple games.

2.00 pm Nappies are checked and changed where needed. Toddlers who are awake are offered water and a healthy snack. They sit in small groups with their key person.

2.15 pm Toddlers go outside with their key person. They play with toys or go for a walk. The adults check for hazards and also supervise children carefully. Staff talk and listen to toddlers.

3.00 pm Some toddlers come indoors. Nappies are checked and changed where necessary. Hands are washed. Children are offered water and a healthy snack if they want one.

A range of toys and resources are put out for toddlers to explore. Staff talk and listen to toddlers.

4.00 pm All toddlers come indoors. Hands are washed. Nappies are checked and changed where necessary. Books, rhymes and simple games are played, if toddlers are interested. Toys and resources are available as well. Drinking water is always available.

Copy and complete this table

Event	How it meets children's basic needs

Read the routine in the table on page 117 carefully and then copy out this table adding some more rows. For every event write down how children's needs are being met.

How everyday activities can promote children's holistic development

We have seen how routines can meet children's care needs and keep them safe. The table below shows how some everyday activities can be used to support children's learning.

Everyday activity	Physical development	Language development	Intellectual development	Social and emotional development
Nap and bedtime	Children learn to dress and undress.	Children talk and share a book to help them relax.	Children learn to recognise time of day and also the difference between day and night.	Children feel reassured and safe as adults say goodnight or help them to fall asleep.
Mealtimes	Children's hand–eye co-ordination is developed by serving food and using cutlery and cups.	As children talk to each other and adults, their language is supported. They also develop words linked with food.	Children learn about tastes and textures as they prepare and try out new foods.	During mealtimes children learn to share, take turns and be with others.
Personal hygiene e.g. handwashing, hair combing and shower/bath time, cleaning teeth	Children's hand–eye co-ordination develops as they learn to join in self-care tasks.	Children learn vocabulary relating to the personal hygiene activity, e.g. 'dry', 'soap'. Children are often talkative as they have time with an adult.	Children learn about germs – things that they cannot see, but can make them poorly. Children also learn as they explore water.	During personal hygiene activities, children can gain confidence as being clean makes them feel good. They can also relax during shower/bath time.
Going for a walk or playing outdoors	Running and walking helps to develop children's hearts and lungs. Physical activity helps children's balance and co-ordination.	Children talk about what they can see and what they have found. Children learn the words for items that they can see outdoors, e.g. 'clouds', 'leaves', 'puddles'.	Children learn about the weather and nature, and how things change. Children can explore different textures and materials.	Children learn to make relationships as they play with others. They can develop confidence as they master physical skills outdoors.

Check what you know

Choose one of the activities in the second table on page 124. Explain how it promotes children's overall development.

Grading

To complete assessment criteria 4.1 and 4.2 and achieve grades D5 D6 A* you will need to:

Describe TWO everyday activities or experiences which support the care needs of children aged from birth to five years and promote their independence, well-being, health and safety.

Describe how these activities and experiences support the children's well-being.

Evaluate how everyday experiences can be used to promote holistic development.

Top marks

In order to get an A1 grade for the assignment for this unit, you will need to show that you can evaluate how everyday experiences can be used to promote activities which contribute to holistic development.

Can you answer the following question:

To what extent do you think that everyday experiences can meet children's basic needs as well as support their development? Give practical examples with your answer.

My life as a nanny

I am a live-in nanny. I am responsible for two children aged 15 months and 3 years. As a live-in nanny, I am there for the children from 7 a.m. in the morning until after bedtime. I have two days off a week. I work closely with the children's parents, and together we have devised the routine of the day for the children. This includes going outdoors everyday as well as nap times and bedtimes.

It is hard work being a nanny and it can also be quite lonely at times as there are often no other adults around. But the children make up for it! I feel part of the family and love watching them develop.

LEARNING OUTCOME 4: UNDERSTAND HOW TO USE EVERYDAY CARE, ROUTINES & ACTIVITIES TO SUPPORT INDEPENDENCE, HEALTH, SAFETY & WELL-BEING

125

■ Learning Outcome 5:
Understand how to support children through transitions in their lives

Learning outcomes	Assessment criteria
The learner will:	The learner can:
5 Understand how to support children through transitions in their lives.	5.1 Describe different transitions that children may experience.
	5.2 Identify the effects of these transitions on holistic development.
	5.3 Describe ways to support children through transitions.

Did you ever move home when you were little? Do you remember starting nursery or school? All children have changes in their lives, which we call **transitions**. In this section we look at the different types of transitions. We also look at how these transitions might affect children, and how early years workers can support children with transitions.

High priority

Make sure you understand the word 'transition'.

Jargon buster

Transition – a change of place, family circumstance and/or of carer.

5.1 Describe different transitions that children may experience

A transition is any change that will be important for a child. This might be a change of environment such as moving home, a change of carer or family circumstance. Transitions may a 'one-off' event, such as going on holiday, or something that will happen regularly, such as going from home to school.

Separating from parents

One of the most important transitions that children make is when they leave their parents or **key carer**. This might be to go to a pre-school, nursery or childminder. As well as changes in carers, children may also have changes to their family circumstances. The table on page 128 shows five of the common transitions where children leave their parent or key carer and five common changes to children's family circumstances.

Why might it be hard for young children to leave their parents?

Separating from parents

Five common transitions where children leave parent/key carer	Five common changes to children's family circumstances
Going to pre-school, nursery, or childminder	Arrival of a new baby
Starting school	Moving home
Being cared for by a family member	Death or illness of a family member
Going to a club or class	Family breakdown e.g. divorce
Changing group or class within a nursery, pre-school or school	Arrival of new step parent and/or step brother and sister

Differences between transitions

Children experience some transitions regularly. They may go every day to a nursery or the home of a family member. These can be easier for children to cope with. Other transitions may be sudden or may only last for a short time. These can be harder for children to manage.

Theory in action

Ben is three years old. He lives with his mother who goes to work. On Mondays and Tuesdays, he goes to a childminder. On Wednesdays, Thursdays and Fridays he goes to a pre-school for the morning. His grandfather picks him up and looks after him in the afternoon. On Saturdays, he stays with his father. On Saturday morning he goes to a swimming class for half an hour. In two weeks' time, he is due to have a minor operation. He will need to stay in hospital for four days. The hospital is near his aunt's flat and he and his mother will stay there the night before.

- Can you count the number of transitions that Kyle has?
- Which transitions are regular ones?

5.2. Identify the effects of these transitions on holistic development

There are many ways in which transitions can affect children's holistic development. The impact on children depends on many things:

- the age of the child
- how well the child is prepared and supported before the transition
- the type of transition
- how well adults work together to support the child during the transition.

Physical development and health

Children's physical development can be affected by transition. They might lack the energy or motivation to make the movements that will support physical development. The spider diagram shows how children's health may be affected by transitions.

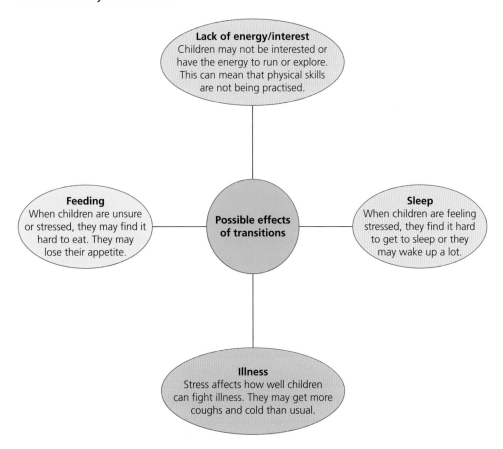

Lack of energy/interest
Children may not be interested or have the energy to run or explore. This can mean that physical skills are not being practised.

Feeding
When children are unsure or stressed, they may find it hard to eat. They may lose their appetite.

Possible effects of transitions

Sleep
When children are feeling stressed, they find it hard to get to sleep or they may wake up a lot.

Illness
Stress affects how well children can fight illness. They may get more coughs and cold than usual.

Check what you know

Why might children move and explore less if they are finding transitions difficult?

Language development

There are many ways in which children's language development can be affected. Here are three possible ways:

- **Wanting to talk** – children who are not sure of a new adult may not want to talk and communicate with them. With children under four years, this can affect how they progress with talking.
- **Finding it hard to listen** – children who are not coping with a transition may find it hard to listen. They may become distracted because they are worried.
- **Withdrawing** – during transitions some children find it hard to be with other children and might want to spend time alone. This means that they are not practising their communication and language skills.

Intellectual development

Intellectual development is about children's memory, concentration and ability to learn. Transitions can have a huge impact on this. Children might find it harder to learn and remember information. Here are three ways in which children's intellectual development can be affected:

- Concentration – how well children learn depends on how well they concentrate. Children who are unhappy or anxious find it hard to pay attention.
- Memory – in order to learn, children have to remember things. Sleep is important for memory. If children are not sleeping well, they might not be able to learn so well.
- Interest – when children are interested, they are more able to learn. Children who are anxious may find it harder to be interested in new toys, resources or activities.

Social and emotional development

When children are unhappy or anxious, it can affect their social and emotional development. As all children are different, they may show that they are stressed in a range of ways. This normally comes out in terms of their behaviours, which can be different at home from in the early years setting. This is why early years workers need to talk to parents about how their child is at home.

Here are five common behaviours that children will often show when they are unhappy or anxious:

- clinginess
- attention-seeking behaviours
- defiance and lack of co-operation
- anger towards others, for example, hitting, spitting, shouting
- withdrawn and lack of interest in others.

How behaviours can affect social and emotional development

When children show any of the above behaviours, it can affect their social and emotional development. They may find that other children will not want to play with them or that adults become cross with them. This in turn can make children feel bad about themselves. This can make them even more unhappy.

Activity

Think about the transitions that you experienced as a child.

- Can you remember how you felt?
- Do you think that they affected your development?

Short-term effects on children

Some transitions can affect children's development, but only in the short term. A good example of this is when a family goes on holiday. While this is a positive transition, the new environment can be unsettling for some young children. They may demand more attention from their parents, and they may not sleep as long as usual because their routine has changed.

Long-term effects on children

Some transitions such as significant changes to family circumstances can have a long-term effect on children. Any situation in which there is conflict between adults often affects development. This is why family breakdown can often cause problems for some children. Long-term effects on children can include difficulty in learning, behaviour and finding friends. The impact on children depends very much on how much support children gain from early years workers, teachers and other adults in their lives.

5.3. Describe ways to support children through transitions

The early years worker has an important role in helping children through transitions. Children are more likely to cope better with transitions when someone they know and trust is helping them through it.

Key person role

Some of the transitions that children experience involve leaving their parent or primary carer. For young children this can be very difficult. The starting point for this type of transition is for the child to develop a relationship with an early years worker in the new setting. Once a child knows this person well, then it is easier for the child to leave their parent or primary carer. This is what is known as a 'key person approach'. It is an approach that is widely used although in some countries the term 'key worker' is used. In England it is a requirement for every early years setting to make sure that children have a key person.

The key person in early years settings will also support children during other transitions such as moving to a new home, starting school or going to a new early years setting. The key person is best placed to do this because they will know the child and the child's parents well.

Check what you know

Explain the role of key person in helping children with transitions.

Preparing children for future transitions

As well as making a relationship with the child, the key person also works closely with the children's parents or primary carers. This means that the key person can help children to prepare for transitions in their lives. Here are four ways in which early years workers might help children prepare for transitions:

- sharing books about the new situation, for example, having a new baby in the family
- visiting a new setting with the child
- planning play activities that link to the transition, for example, creating a dressing-up box about hospitals
- showing photographs of the new carer or environment and allowing the child to ask questions.

Supporting children during transitions

When children are going through a transition, the adult who is the key person is best placed to support them. There are several different kinds of support:

Good communication

Children need opportunities to talk about how they are feeling and also to ask questions. It is important to follow the child's lead. This means being a good listener but also not making children talk if they do not want to. It is also important to tell children the truth about what is happening. This might include saying that you do not know.

For younger children, the early years worker might need to simplify what they say. Some activities can help children talk more about how they are feeling:

- sharing books or making books about the situation
- using puppets or dolls as props to talk about feelings and what is happening.

Providing play opportunities

Children can often express their feelings and make sense of what is happening through play. Activities that help children express their feelings include sensory activities. Here are some common sensory activities that might help children express their feelings (which might also include anger):

- dough
- sand
- water
- painting
- musical instruments.

Early years workers can also support children through setting up role play. Role play can help children to act out what is happening to them. This can help them to make sense of the situation. Role play might include home corner, props for a hospital or long journey.

Providing reassurance

The early years worker will also need to provide reassurance for children. Younger children often need physical reassurance and will want to hold hands or have a hug. Older children might need to know that whatever happens, they are still loved.

Early years workers can also provide reassurance by being positive in their body language. This means greeting children with a smile and being patient with them. Children can also be reassured if there is a good routine in place. This is very important as children can feel more secure when they know what to expect and what will be happening next.

Extend

Visit this website to learn more about how to help children who are experiencing a significant transition – going into Great Ormond Street Hospital for treatment: www.gosh.nhs.uk/parents-and-visitors/advice-when-you-stay/coping-hospital-visit/helping-your-child-cope.

Grading

In order to achieve assessment criteria 5.1 and 5.2 and also to achieve grading criteria D7 C1 B1, you will need to:

Identify different transitions that children may experience

and

how children's development may be affected when they experience transitions.

Describe ways the early years worker can support children through transitions.

My life as a pre-school assistant

I work at a pre-school. We take children from two years until they start school. Most of the children attend each weekday for three hours, although parents can choose whether they come in the morning or the afternoon.

I am a key person to six children. Being a key person is quite a responsibility as you have to be able to develop a good relationship with parents as well as the children. The relationship with children begins when they come for settling-in visits. We have a very good settling-in system here. We take our time and build a relationship with children first, before parents leave. This means that we have happy children who enjoy coming from day one. This is important as for many of our children, it will be the first time that they have left their families.

In some ways being a key person is about being there for children. It might be that children need a cuddle, want to show me something that they have done or want me to come and play with them. It is also my role to help them prepare for going to school. We look at books, but I also go up with them to their school and visit their new teacher. The new teacher also comes to our pre-school. This helps children to feel more comfortable and get used to the idea of moving on. So far in my career, I have always managed to build a strong relationship with children. I even think about my key children on my day off!

Unit 3

Childcare and development 0–5 years

About this unit

This unit is a revision of the knowledge you have covered when learning about childcare and development of children aged from birth to five years. In this unit you will look at the requirements of the Multiple Choice Question (MCQ) paper which you need in order to be successful in completing your qualification. You will need to know and understand what to expect in the paper as well as being clear on the knowledge you need to have. This includes understanding how children develop, thinking about their individual needs, and knowing about your responsibilities when learning about how to work with children.

In this unit we will look carefully at the format of the MCQ paper, and then go through the key points which you will need to revise so that you can ensure you have the knowledge you need to complete the paper and achieve your award.

The format of the MCQ paper

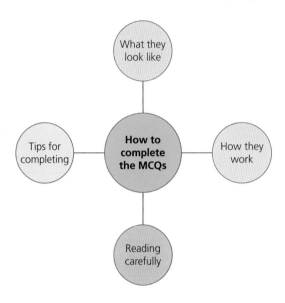

What they look like

It will be helpful for you to have some practice in looking at and completing multiple choice questions in the format they will be presented to you, so that you are prepared for the MCQ paper. In order to complete the paper, you will have both a question book and an answer sheet.

How they work

MCQs usually have four possible answers. You will need to read through each of these and then choose *one* by carefully eliminating those which are incorrect.

You will then need to choose *one* answer on the answer sheet. Your answer must be clear, so if you make any mistakes or change your mind, make sure you rub them out thoroughly so that it is easy to see which one you think is correct.

Read carefully

Because they are short, there is sometimes a temptation with MCQs to answer them quickly; you should try not to do this. Read each question and each possible answer carefully so that you can make sure you have not missed anything. You will be looking at how to work through the possibilities for the answers in 'Step by step' below.

Tips for completing

Make sure you are prepared for the test and have all the things you need with you. These will include a ruler, a rubber and a sharpened HB pencil.

It may be helpful when you are reading the questions to hold the ruler beneath each line as you read it so that you stay focused on the text. When you are completing the question and you have read the text carefully, you will need to make a mark on the paper.

Step by step: Completing a question

It can be helpful to look at an MCQ step by step. Here is an example of a question:

1   A child's emotional development will be *most* affected by:
    a) losing a toy
    b) visit of a grandparent
    c) birth of a sibling
    d) grazing a knee

In this example, the key words are emotional development and 'most'.

As grazing a knee is more likely to affect children's physical development, this answer can be eliminated.

Now we are left with three possible answers:
    a) losing a toy
    b) visit of a grandparent
    c) birth of a sibling

While children will be upset if they lose a toy, there is no mention that this is a favourite toy or a comforter. This means that a child is likely to be upset only in the short term. The question looks at children's longer term development. This cannot be the answer.

You are now left with two possible answers and need to make a choice as to which one will have the most impact (affect) on the child's emotional development.

While both are important, the correct answer will be the **birth of a sibling** as it is also more of a long-term change. This is because the new baby and the child will be growing up together and a new baby will change the family situation considerably.

Activity

Identifying key words

Look at the start to these three questions. Underline the key words in each of them.

- At four years most children can …
- An adult can best help a two-year-old's physical development by …
- How can an early years worker best help a two-year-old during a transition?

■ Learning Outcome 1: Understand the stages of development of children aged 0–5 years

Learning outcomes	Assessment criteria
The learner will:	The learner can:
Understand the stages of development of children aged 0–5 years.	1.1.1 Describe the main areas of development of children aged 0–5 years.
	1.1.2 Outline the stages of development of children aged 0–5 years.
	1.1.3 Identify methods for observing children
	1.1.4 Identify reasons for observing children's holistic development.

1.1 Describe the main areas of development of children aged 0–5 years

For this learning outcome, you will need to understand what skills and knowledge are in each of the learning areas. You will also need to know how each area of development links together. This is called holistic development.

In Unit 2 we looked at the way that development is split into four main areas:

- physical
- language
- intellectual
- social and emotional.

Areas of development – fill in the blanks

Physical development	Movement, balance and co-ordination
	Talking, listening and understanding Reading and writing for older children
Intellectual development	
Social and emotional development	Relationships with others, managing feelings, confidence and self-control

In preparation for the test you will also need to know more about each of the areas of development. Let's look at each of the areas of development and revise what is in them.

Physical development

This is all about movement, but there are two broad types of movements that children make – fine motor movements and gross motor movements:

- *Fine motor movements* are small movements, usually made with the hands.
- *Gross motor movements* are larger movements that involve moving the whole arm or leg.

Test yourself

To check that you know the types of movements, give two examples of:

- a fine motor movement
- a gross motor movement.

Explain what type of movement this child is making

Resources and activities for physical development

In order to promote children's physical development, there are some resources and activities that most early years settings will use. The table at the top of page 140 shows examples of resources for different age groups, although what might be chosen for a child will depend on their stage of development. Look at these before you take your exam, and also consider other resources that might support physical development for different ages and stages of children.

Resources and activities for physical development

Age	Fine motor development	Gross motor development
0–1 years	Rattles Soft toys	Baby activity mat Baby gym
1–2 years	Pop-up toys Stacking beakers	Push and pull toys Brick trolley Sit and ride toy Swing
2–3 years	Jigsaw puzzles Painting Sand and water play Large wooden bricks	Rocking horse Ball Sit and ride toy Tricycle without pedals
3–5 years	Sand and water play Construction bricks Sewing cards	Bat and ball Climbing frame Tricycle Hoops

Activity

Look at a toy catalogue for physical development.

- For each age group, look at the type of resources and toys available.
- Choose two items for each age group.
- Explain why these may benefit children's physical development.

Language development

This is about how we communicate. There are many skills including talking, listening and understanding. In older children, it is also about learning to read and write.

Test yourself

Do you know the terms used in language development? See if you can fill in the blanks in the table below.

Language development – fill in the blanks

Receptive language	Words and phrases that children understand
	Words and phrases that children can say
Facial expression, e.g. eye contact, frowning	
	Communication using the body, e.g. gestures with hands, shrug of shoulder, turning back

Resources and activities – language development

Many resources and activities are used across the age ranges to promote children's language development. Here are some examples of these:

- sharing books including picture books and flap books
- resources for drawing and **mark-making** from one year such as paints, pens and crayons
- puppets including glove puppets and finger puppets
- songs and rhymes including finger rhymes and action rhymes.

> ### Jargon buster
>
> **Mark-making** – A stage before children learn to write when they explore making marks with pens, paints and other resources.

Which area of development is being supported in this photo?

Activity

Look on the internet or in a book for an example of:

- an action rhyme
- a finger rhyme.

Intellectual development

This is about we think, learn and use information. Intellectual development is used to help us organise, problem-solve and also remember information.

> ### Test yourself
>
> Choose two tasks from the list that require high levels of intellectual development:
>
> - completing a jigsaw puzzle
> - drinking from a cup
> - playing a card game
> - putting on a coat.
>
> For each task, explain the skills that are needed that link to intellectual development.

Resources and activities to support intellectual development

Intellectual development is a complex area, but there are some types of resources and activities that an early years setting might use to support this area of development.

Resources and activities to support intellectual development

Sand and water play	Texture
	Learning about measuring and volume by filling containers
	Learning by trial and error about properties of sand/water
Jigsaw puzzles	Learning about shape and size
	Problem-solving and logic
Construction play	Learning how to build structures
	Learning about shape and measuring
	Learning by trial and error about how to join and build structures
	Learning how to problem-solve and plan
Board and card games, e.g. snap, snakes and ladders	Opportunity to practise counting
	Opportunity to match shapes, colours or pictures
	Learning strategy

Social and emotional development

There are two aspects within this area of development. They are closely linked, but they are slightly different:

- *Social development* is about our relationships with others.
- *Emotional development* is about our feelings and emotions.

Test yourself

Sort out the following into examples of either social or emotional development:

- feeling sad
- playing with a friend
- having a tantrum
- copying what someone else is doing
- taking turns during a game.

Resources and activities to support social and emotional development

There are a few resources and activities that early years settings will provide that will help children's social and emotional development.

Supporting social and emotional development

Snack and mealtime	Help children to talk and be together
	Encourage children to take turns and share
Role play/dressing up	Encourage children to play together
	Children explore what it is like to be someone else
	Children play out things that have happened to them
Musical activities	Help children to express their emotions
	As part of a group, children can join in and gain a sense of belonging
Painting and creative activities	Help children to express their emotions
	Children can feel proud of what they have made or created

Holistic development

The term 'holistic development' is used to talk about how the different areas of development work together. You will need to know how the areas of development are linked together. We looked at this on pages xx–xx in Unit 2.

Theory in action

Holistic development

Michael is four years old. His language is significantly delayed. He tends to play alone as he cannot join in with the other children who use a lot of language as they play. The early years workers have noticed that he still has tantrums. They think that this is linked to frustration as he cannot always say what he wants or needs. While other children of his age are using a lot of different play equipment, Michael tends to prefer playing with the same resources. His play is quite repetitive.

- How is Michael's language delay affecting his social development?
- Explain how Michael's intellectual development might be affected because he tends to play with the same resources.
- Describe how Michael's emotional development is linked to his language delay.

Test yourself

Holistic development

See the table on page 144. For each area of development, give two different ways in which it can support other areas of development. Physical development has been done as an example.

Holistic development – fill in the blanks

Physical development	
Intellectual development	Children can learn more if they are able to move and explore
Social development	Children who can move and use their hands will find it easier to play with others
Language development	
Intellectual development	
Social and emotional development	

Test time

If you understand the skills within each of the areas of development, you should be able to answer these questions. Make sure that you read the question very carefully.

1 Which of these activities would best support a five-year-old's gross motor movement?

a) Using a climbing frame

b) Listening to a story

c) Singing a nursery rhyme

d) Drinking from a cup

2 Which of these activities would best promote a three-year-old's social development?

a) Playing in the sand alone

b) Looking at a book

c) Joining in with songs

d) Playing a computer game

3 Problems with language development can affect children's:

a) Ability to put on a coat

b) Ability to play with other children

c) Ability to play in the sand

d) Ability to climb

1.2 Outline the stages of development of children aged 0–5 years

You will need to spend quite a lot of time revising the stages of development for children that we looked at in Unit 2. There might be several questions that require you to know the typical development of children. Here is an example of a question

1 At 18 months, most children can:
   a) Throw a ball accurately
   b) Kick a ball with force
   c) Stand and walk
   d) Crawl and stand

Remembering the milestones across the four areas of development and for each age group is going to be quite a challenge. The best way is to keep revising, using a range of different methods. Let's look at each area of development and see what you can remember.

Physical development

A good starting point is to look at the stages by which babies are likely to become mobile. This follows a clear sequence. For each photograph, see if you can work out how old the baby is likely to be.

This baby is sitting up but needs support. How old?

This baby can sit up without help and can reach for a toy. How old?

This baby can walk but holds onto furniture. How old?

Most children are confidently walking at this age. How old?

Patterns of physical development

You will need to learn the age at which children are likely to acquire different physical skills. We looked at this on pages 65–71.

We looked at this on pages 65–71.

Test yourself

Copy and complete the table below. For each age, give one example of a fine and a gross motor skill that is typical.

Fine and gross motor skills – fill in the blanks

Age	Fine motor	Gross motor
1–2 years		
2–3 years		
3–5 years		

Activity

Make up a physical development quiz to try out on your friends.

Create ten true or false questions about children's gross and fine motor skills. Here are two to get you started:
1 Most children at three years are out of nappies.
2 Most children at 18 months have a preferred hand.

Answers are on the next page.

Answers to the Activity on page 146:
1 True
2 False

Language development

You need to know the sequence by which children learn to talk. This includes the age at which babies first start to recognise words and make gestures as well as the age at which children start to talk well.

Babies – birth to one year

The first year of language development is about babies learning the skills of communication and learning to associate sounds with words. This means that few babies are actually using any words, although they might be starting to recognise some from around nine months.

Test yourself

Use the table below to answer these questions:

- At what age are most babies turning to look at a speaker's face?
- At what age will babies babble in long strings, for example, babab babababa?
- At what age are most babies able to follow simple questions?

Expressive and receptive language milestones

Age	Expressive language	Receptive language
6 weeks	Coos	Recognises parent's voice and calms down if crying Turns to look at speaker's face
3 months	Makes happy sounds when spoken to	Can be soothed quickly when adult talks and holds baby
6 months	Babbles with repeated sounds: dah-dah; ba-ba Laughs and chuckles when happy	Turns to look at parent if hears voice across the room
9 months	Makes sounds to gain attention Babbling becomes longer: babadada; dadadadada Baby will babble when alone	Understands 2 or 3 phrases used frequently by adults, e.g. 'no' and 'bye-bye'
12 months	Babbling is tuneful and in long strings Raises voice to gain attention	Can follow simple instructions, e.g. 'Give me the spoon' Understands words used frequently in routines, e.g. 'cup', 'spoon', 'go for a walk'

Language development for toddlers and young children

You will need to pinpoint some of the language milestones for children aged from one to five years. Let's look at some examples of key milestones.

Expressive language:

- Using single words – at 18 months, most toddlers are using single words (6–20 words).
- Two-word sentences – at two years, most toddlers are starting to join two words, for example, 'dada gone'.
- Uses simple questions – at two-and-a-half years, children can say simple questions, such as 'What's dat?'
- Speech mainly clear – at three years, most of what is said can be understood by others.
- Fluent language – at four years.

Test yourself

Receptive language

Can you put ages next to these key milestones?

- Can point to several parts of the body.
- Understands most of what adults say to him or her.
- Can follow instructions in two parts, for example, 'Find Teddy's hat and put it on him'.
- Knows several nursery rhymes.
- Loves hearing and making up jokes.

Intellectual development

You will need to make sure that you understand what skills and knowledge link to intellectual development. On pages 78–82 we looked at some of the typical tasks that children at different ages are able to complete.

Test yourself

Try out your knowledge of children's pattern of development by trying out this True or False quiz:

- Most babies at three months will look for a hidden object (object permanence).
- Most two-year-olds can complete a jigsaw with 12 pieces.
- Most four-year-olds will recognise and name the colours red, blue and green.
- Most three-year-olds will be able to copy a circle.
- Most five-year-olds can count to 20.

Social and emotional development

This is an area which lends itself well to MCQ questions. Let's look at a few aspects that you should particularly revise.

Attachment and bonding

This is about the way that babies and young children develop a strong relationship with their parents or main carers. We looked at this on pages 82–87. It is worth revising this.

> **Test yourself**
>
> Can you answer these questions:
> - At what age do children start to be uncomfortable when they are held by a stranger?
> - At what age do children start to cry if they cannot see their parent or key carer?

Friendships and play

How children play together depends on their social development. There are three terms that are used to describe the way that children play together:

- solitary play – where children play alone
- parallel play – where children play alongside each other
- co-operative play – where children play together.

> **Test yourself**
>
> We looked at parallel and co-operative play in Unit 2.
> - At what age are children likely to show co-operative play?

Behaviour

Children's social and emotional development is also reflected in their behaviour. You might be asked about this. Read the sections on social and emotional behaviour carefully and look out for points about how children may behave.

> **Test yourself**
>
> Can you answer these questions:
> - What age is associated with tantrums?
> - What might be the reason for tantrums?
> - At what age can most children take turns and share?

The role of adults in supporting the areas of development

We have already looked at the resources that might be used to support children's development, but you might be asked about the role of adults in supporting development. We looked at some of the ways that adults can help children in Unit 2 and you should revise these. In addition, here are some other tips.

Physical development:

- Provide resources that link to children's stage of development.
- Encourage children to have a go by standing near them or breaking a task down into steps.
- Observe children's stage of development and plan appropriate activities.
- Talk to children about potential risks and help them to manage hazards.

Language development:

- Make eye contact and get down to children's level.
- Talk to babies and children.
- Respond to babies and children positively.
- Share books with babies and children.
- Sing nursery rhymes with children.

Intellectual development:

- Provide opportunities for problem-solving.
- Point out things of interest to children, for example, colours, shapes, textures.
- Accurately name objects.
- Accurately explain concepts when they occur, for example, weather, colours.
- Use everyday routines to help children become aware of number, for example, counting steps, counting out plates and beakers.

Social and emotional development:

- Use words to help children understand how they are feeling, for example, you look sad.
- Encourage children to talk about how they are feeling.
- Recognise that behaviour will be affected by stage of development, for example, tantrums at two years.
- Support children under three years to take turns and share.
- Praise children for being kind or thoughtful.

At what age are children likely to have tantrums?

Activity

Using information from Unit 2 and the tips that we have looked at, create a leaflet that explains how adults can support children's development in each of the areas of development.

Test time

See how well you do in answering these questions that look at the pattern of development, but also how adults might support development.

1 Most babies at nine months are

   a) Saying five words

   b) Cooing and smiling

   c) Responding to a few words

   d) Starting to babble

2 Most three-year-olds can

   a) Dress themselves

   b) Ride a tricycle

   c) Skip to music

   d) Stand on one foot

3 How can adults best support social development in children aged three years?

   a) Praise children who are playing alone

   b) Remind children to say please and thank you

   c) Plan a group storytime

   d) Encourage children to talk at mealtimes

4 At what age are most children able to play co-operatively?

   a) 0–1 years

   b) 1–2 years

   c) 2–3 years

   d) 3–4 years

5 An example of intellectual development for a child aged four years includes

   a) Completing a three-piece jigsaw puzzle

   b) Riding a tricycle

   c) Counting five objects

   d) Putting a coat on

1.3 Identify methods for observing children

In Unit 2, we looked at methods for observing children. In preparation for the MCQ paper, you will need to know about different methods for observing children and why they are used. You will also need to know the advantages and disadvantages of each. Let's begin by revising the main types of observation methods – see the first table.

Different types of observation method

Method	Action
Narrative methods	Observer writes down what they can see at the time.
Checklist/tickchart	Observer has certain things to look out for or tasks for the child to complete.
Time sample	Observer records what the child is doing regularly over a period of time, e.g. every 10 minutes over 2 hours.
Event sample	A record is kept every time a child shows a certain behaviour, e.g. biting or tantrum.
Sociogram	Children are asked about who they like to play with.

Advantages and disadvantages of observation methods

Activity

Copy and complete this table, writing down the advantages and disadvantages of each observation method.

Method	Advantage	Disadvantage
Narrative methods		
Checklist/tickchart		
Time sample		
Event sample		
Sociogram		

Reasons for using different observation methods

Some types of observation methods are used for particular reasons. Make sure that you remember the following:

- event samples – mainly used to record children's behaviour
- sociogram – mainly used to record children's friendships.

It is also worth remembering that the other observation methods can be used to record a wide range of children's development.

Confidentiality

You may be asked a question about confidentiality and the importance of keeping observation and records secure. We looked at this in Unit 2 on page 89. You will need to revise this.

Accuracy

Accuracy is important when observing children. This is because the information gained may be used to plan further activities or to feed back to parents and other professionals. If information is not accurate, children might not be given the support that they need, or the activities that are planned may not meet the children's developmental needs. We looked at the importance of accuracy on page 90. It might be worth revising this.

Test time

See if you can answer the following questions:

1 An early years worker is most likely to use an event sample to understand a child's
   a) Friendships
   b) Physical development
   c) Unwanted behaviour
   d) Language development

2 It is most important that all observations include
   a) The name of the child's parents
   b) The date and time
   c) What the child was wearing
   d) The child's favourite toy

1.4 Identify reasons for observing children's holistic development

In Unit 2, we looked at the many reasons why it is important to look at children's holistic development. We also saw that the information gained from observations might also be shared with a wide range of people. You will need to read pages 88–101 and revise these.

Reasons for observing development

Reasons for observing development	Why this is important
Checking the pattern of children's development	
Planning to support development and children's interests	
Understanding children's behaviour	To see if there are any reasons why children are showing unwanted behaviour.
Sharing information with parents	
Providing information to professionals	To help children when they move setting as the new early years worker will know more about their needs and interests.
	To help other professionals such as a speech and language therapist know about the child's development and behaviour when they are in the early years setting.

Activity

Read pages 98–101 and then see if you can fill in this table. Two answers have already been provided.

Check what you know

Can you explain why it is important that information to be shared with others is always accurate?

Test time

1 In order to plan an activity for a child the early years worker should **first**

   a) Observe the child's development

   b) Check that there are enough toys

   c) Wash the child's hands

   d) Talk to the child's friend

2 When sharing observations with other professionals it is **most** important that

   a) The observations are about social development

   b) The observations are up to date and accurate

   c) The observations include children's friendships

   d) The observations include photographs

■ Learning Outcome 2: Understand factors that may affect children's development

As part of your revision for the MCQ paper, you will need to know about factors that may affect children's development. In this section we look at factors that contribute towards children's development, transition and also the importance of inclusive practice.

Learning outcome	Assessment criteria
The learner will:	The learner can:
2 Understand factors that may affect children's development.	2.1 Identify factors which may contribute to children's development.
	2.2 Describe how factors can affect children's development.
	2.3 Describe transitions that children may experience and the effects these may have on the child.
	2.4 Explain ways to support children during transitions.
	2.5 Explain the importance of being fair, equal and inclusive towards children.

In order to achieve success on the MCQ paper, you will need to know about the factors that can affect children's development. These include children's transitions and also the importance of inclusive practice. You will need to revise pages xx–xx of Unit 1 as well as pages xx–xx of Unit 2.

2.1 Identify factors which may contribute to children's development

You will need to know about the wide range of factors that can affect children's development. In Unit 2, we divided these into personal and external factors. Remember to revise factors that contribute positively to children's development, as well as those that might cause problems.

Check what you know

Can you remember the difference between personal and external factors?

Different factors affecting development

Personal factors

Personal factors are those that are unique to the child and are either inherited or occurred during pregnancy. You will need to identify a range of these factors. Read pages 102–103 and then try the following Test yourself.

Test yourself

Which of these are personal factors affect development?
- having asthma
- going to a pre-school
- being the tallest child in the class
- having a lot of toys

External factors

These are the events and experiences during childhood. There are many factors that fit into this category. They include where children live, whether they go to nursery or another early years setting and also whether they are happy at home and in school.

We looked at some of the external factors on pages 103–104.

Test yourself

Can you think of two external factors that might affect children's development?

Factors that might positively contribute towards development

It is important to be able to identify some factors that can positively contribute towards children's development. Let's look at some of these here.

- **Stimulation and play** – children need plenty of different opportunities to explore and play. Children who go to early years settings will have a wide range of opportunities for both stimulation and play.
- **Food and drink** – children need food and drink as part of a balanced diet so that they can grow and develop.
- **Love and interaction** – children need plenty of opportunities to feel loved by parents and key carers. They also need opportunities to talk and communicate.
- **Physical conditions** – children need to be kept safe and also warm. This means their physical needs can be met and also they can stay safe. You should also revise some of children's basic needs as these also link to children's development. We looked at these on page 104 of Unit 2.

Factors that negatively affect development

While we have looked in general at factors affecting development, you should also be aware of some factors that can negatively affect children's development. Look back at Unit 2 and read pages 102–107.

Check what you know

Make a list of negative factors that might negatively affect children's development.

Test time

1 What may **most** affect the holistic development of a child aged three years?

   a) Attending a pre-school

   b) Watching a lot of television

   c) Playing alone with sand and water

   d) Having music lessons

2 Stimulating activities are most important for children's holistic development to

   a) Keep them busy

   b) Prevent squabbles

   c) Help them learn

   d) Help them make friends

2.2 Describe how factors can affect children's development

We have seen that there are many factors that affect children's development. In preparation for the MCQ paper, you will need to be able to recognise how individual factors might impact children's holistic development, as well as individual areas of development.

Let's start off by looking at how some of the personal factors that we looked at on pages 102–103 may affect children's development. Read the table on page 102 carefully and then have a go at the Test yourself.

Test yourself

Explain how a medical condition might affect a child's intellectual and social development.

External factors

What happens to children after they are born can contribute towards their development. We looked at external factors on pages 103–104. Revise this again and then see if you can answer the questions in this Test yourself.

Test yourself

Can you link external factors to children's development?
- Explain how stimulation and interaction can affect children's intellectual and language development.
- Explain the importance of a balanced diet for children's development.

Negative factors

We saw in Unit 2 how negative factors such as bereavement, family breakdown and also poverty can negatively affect a child's development. Revise this section carefully.

Test yourself

How might the development of a child who has been bullied or discriminated against be affected?

Positive and negative factors affecting areas of development

Area of development	Positive factor	Negative factor
Physical development	Healthy and balanced diet	Lack of opportunity to exercise
Language development		
Intellectual development		
Social development		
Emotional development		

Check what you know

Look at the table above. For each area of development, write one factor that might affect a child's development positively and one factor that might affect it negatively.

Test time

See if you can answer these questions. Remember that factors can affect children's development both positively and negatively. Make sure that you read the questions and answers carefully.

1 What will most contribute towards a child's language development?
   a) Plenty of exercise
   b) Talking with an adult
   c) Having a balanced diet
   d) Counting ten objects

2 What will most contribute towards a child's social development?
   a) Playing with other children
   b) Being told to share
   c) Using a swing
   d) Washing hands

3 What will most affect a child's intellectual development?
   a) Being given the same toys and activities
   b) Being told to share nicely
   c) Being able to dress independently
   d) Being able to use a knife and fork

4 Going to an early years setting can boost social development because
   a) Children have opportunities to play together
   b) Children can use a wide range of resources
   c) Children are encouraged to count
   d) Children learn to be independent

2.3 Describe transitions that children may experience and the effects these may have on the child

We looked at different types of transitions in Unit 2. Transitions play an important role in children's development. A transition is any change to a child's life. This can be a change of key carer or setting such as when children move between home and school. It can also be a more significant transition such as when a child's family circumstances change. Transitions can have long-and short-term effects on children's development.

In the MCQ paper you will need to recognise different types of transitions and also know about the type of effects they may have on children's development.

Let's start by going back to page 126 and revising the different types of transitions that involve children changing key carer.

Check what you know

Explain what is meant by a transition.

Test yourself

Write down three transitions where children will be leaving their parents or key carer.

This child is coming to nursery/pre-school for the first time. Why is this a significant transition?

Changes to family circumstances

Children might have changes to their family circumstances. These can be very significant. Make sure that you can identify several examples of these. If you are not sure, go back to page 128.

Test time

1 Which of these are **not** examples of changes in family circumstances?
   a) Moving home
   b) Going to school
   c) Parents separating
   d) Playing in the park

Effects on development

As well as identifying different types of transition, you will also need to be confident about how transitions can affect children's development. Begin by looking at how transitions may affect children's physical development and health. You can find this on pages 128–129 in Unit 2.

Test yourself

Can you complete this spider diagram that shows how transitions can affect physical development and health? One has been completed for you

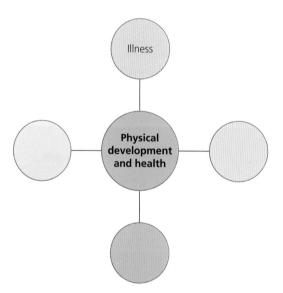

Language development

Some children's language development can be affected during transitions. They may not want to talk to new adults or the other children. Revise how language development can be affected on page 129 and then see if you can answer the Test yourself.

Intellectual development

We looked at how transitions can affect children's ability to think, remember and concentrate. In particular we saw that there were three key potential effects on intellectual development on page 130.

Social and emotional development

Children's social and emotional development is often the area where most impact is seen when a transition takes place. If there is a question about transition, and you are unsure about which answer to choose, remember that social and emotional development is the key area that is likely to be affected. In particular children often show a range of behaviours that indicate that they are under stress. We looked at this on pages 130–131. You will need to revise this carefully.

1 A key person helps a child during transition by
   a) Telling them the rules
   b) Offering reassurance
   c) Putting out play activities
   d) Making the child share

2 Moving to a new nursery is likely to affect children's
   a) Physical development
   b) Intellectual development
   c) Language development
   d) Emotional development

3 What will **most** affect a child's emotional development?
   a) Walking every day
   b) Separation of parents
   c) Having a bedtime story
   d) Playing with a cuddly toy

4 A common transition for young children is
   a) Going to the park
   b) Going to a nursery
   c) Having new toys
   d) Playing with friends

2.4 Explain ways to support children during transitions

As well as identifying transitions and recognising the impact on children's development, you will also need to know the practical ways in which children can be supported. You should understand the role of the key person. In early years settings this is the person who takes time to build a strong relationship with a child and their family, and so helps children during transitions.

A good starting point when looking at how best to support children during transitions is to revise pages 131–133 in Unit 2.

Preparing children for transition

You will need to know some practical ways that early years workers or key persons can prepare children in advance of a transition. Some of these practical strategies can also be used during transition too. It is worth remembering this in case a question comes up and you are not sure of the answer. On page 132, we looked at four ways that you might support children ahead of a transition.

Can you complete this spider diagram by suggesting three other ways to prepare a child for a transition?

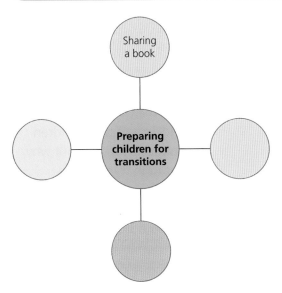

Supporting children during transitions

In this section in Unit 2, we found many strategies that early years workers can use to support children during transitions. You will need to read this section very carefully. Begin by looking at good communication.

Test yourself

Read the section on good communication. See if you can answer the following True or False questions:

1 Children should not be given opportunities to talk about their feelings.
2 Children should be encouraged to ask questions.
3 An early years worker should follow children's lead and be a good listener.
4 An early years worker should encourage children to talk even if they do not want to.
5 An early years worker should tell children the truth.
6 An early years worker may need to simplify what is happening for older children.
7 A good activity to help children talk about transition is using puppets.

Providing play opportunities

In Unit 2, we also looked at the importance of play opportunities for children who are going through a transition. Some of the play opportunities that work well allow children to express their feelings. Read page 133 and see if you can then answer the Test yourself.

Providing reassurance

Another way of supporting children during transitions is to provide reassurance. In Unit 2 we looked at the importance of children being given physical reassurance. This would usually be done by the child's key person as they will have a strong relationship with the child. In addition, children can also find reassurance through routines. Read page 133 to find out why routines are important when children are going through transitions.

2.5 Explain the importance of being fair, equal and inclusive towards children

In Unit 1, we looked at the importance of being fair, equal and inclusive towards all children. You will need to know exactly what 'inclusive practice' means so that you can show that you follow it. There is a definition of inclusive practice on page 26, but before you go and look at it, see if you can answer the following 'True or False' examples.

There is a definition of inclusive practice on page 26

Test yourself

True or False – the following are examples of inclusive practice:
1 Displaying the work of all children.
2 Stopping children from doing activities if you don't think they will be able to.
3 Letting the boys run around outside because you think they need it more.
4 Involving all cultures and languages in the life of the setting.
5 Removing barriers that might prevent children from being involved.
6 Making sure that you treat all children fairly.
7 Giving every child the same opportunities.

Why is it important for settings to demonstrate inclusive practice?

Content on main areas of inclusive practice

In the section on page 43 we looked at how we can ensure that we involve all children fairly and equally in all areas of learning and development. It is very important for all children to feel that they are included and valued so that they can learn and develop to the best of their ability. By limiting their opportunities, we may prevent them from doing this without knowing we are doing it, due to our own **prejudice**, or assumptions about what they are able to do. This is called **discrimination** and we may do it for different reasons.

In the section on page 43

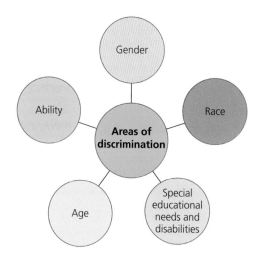

- **Gender** – assuming that only boys or girls can take part in certain activities. For example, many boys enjoy playing with the cars and trucks but this does not mean that girls do not enjoy playing with them, or that they should be prevented from doing so.
- **Race** – having stereotypical assumptions about what some cultures or races may be good at or be able to do. For example, thinking that because a child is from China that they will be good with numbers, or because a child is German that they will be very organised. This is a clear example of prejudice because we are making an assumption which is not based on a fact.
- **SEND** – thinking that you know what a child with SEND may or may not be able to do without checking first.

Theory in action

Mandy is working in a nursery class with Suzie, a child that she knows has some mobility issues due to spina bifida. She is taking the children outside in small groups to do some planting and has left Suzie until last as she is not sure how she will manage, particularly with the steps down to the planters. Now she is not sure what to do.

- What could Mandy have done before starting the activity with the children?
- What can she do now?

- **Age** – thinking that children of a particular age might not be able to do something, based on what you know about that age rather than what you know about the child. For example, assuming that a child of 18 months will not be able to kick a ball and therefore not giving them the opportunity.

Extend

Explain the difference between prejudice and discrimination.

Test yourself

Give **two** reasons why it is important to include all children in all areas of learning and development.

- **Ability** – not allowing children of higher or lesser ability to try activities which will challenge them, because you think they are too easy or that they will not be able to do them.

Theory in action

Jamal is playing 'Kim's game' a memory game with Ryan, a three-year-old who is very quick at remembering the different items. Ryan's friend, Sammy, has come over and has asked if he can play too. Jamal tells him that it is a game just for Ryan but that he can watch if he likes.

- Why would it be a good idea for Jamal to include Sammy?
- How will Sammy feel if he is excluded from the activity?

When you are working with children, make sure that you avoid making any assumptions about them and what they are able to do. Always encourage children positively so that they are more likely to 'have a go' and try new things: this in turn will develop their confidence.

Test time

1 Which of the following is **not** a reason to include all children in activities?

   a) It makes them feel valued

   b) It makes them respect diversity

   c) It makes their parents happy

   d) It makes them more inclusive themselves

2 Early years workers can give equal opportunities to all children by

   a) Putting children's names on everything

   b) Making sure all activities are accessible

   c) Making sure all children complete all activities

   d) Letting all children sit with their friends

3 Which of these is discrimination?

   a) Giving children snacks at different times

   b) Only letting girls in the role play area

   c) Having books which involve all cultures

   d) Celebrating different religious festivals

■ Learning Outcome 3:
Know the variety of provision available for children in different sectors

Assessment criteria grid

Learning outcomes The learner will:	Assessment criteria The learner can:
3 Know the variety of provision available for children in different sectors.	3.1 Describe a variety of provision available for children.

In this section we looked at the different kinds of settings and provision which are available to children, the age groups they are suitable for and the way in which they are funded.

Test yourself

As a starting point for your revision, see how many different types of childcare settings you can list.

Now have a look at the table on page 3 to check your answers.

What age group is a nursery suitable for?'

3.1 Describe a variety of provision available for children

Content on the different types of provision

For the MCQ paper, you will need to know in detail about the types of settings and provision which are available so that you can describe them. Not all of these settings will work with children between the ages of birth and five years, so you will also need to know about the specific ages of the children for which the different provision is suitable.

Voluntary sector provision

These are settings which are run and funded by voluntary contributions. Examples of voluntary sector provision might be:

- a parent and toddler group run by volunteers
- playgroups
- other groups which are not given any outside funding.

Hours are likely to be short and parents might need to stay with their children.

Private sector provision

This is provision that parents and carers pay for as it is run privately. It may be a crèche, a workplace nursery or with a childminder. This kind of childcare will be flexible and more hours will usually be available, depending on what is needed.

Statutory provision

This is provision which is funded by the government. It will include settings such as schools and children's centres. Hours will usually be set and may only run in term time.

Test yourself

Can you fill in the table below with some examples of different provision and the ages of the children they are suitable for?

Different types of childcare provision and appropriate ages

Voluntary sector provision	Private sector provision	Statutory provision	Age of children

Test time

1 A type of private sector provision for young children is a
   a) Playgroup
   b) Childminder
   c) Nursery class in a school
   d) Children's centre

2 Parents would be able to leave a one-year-old child unaccompanied at a
   a) Parent and toddler group
   b) Children's centre
   c) Home-based childcare setting
   d) School-based nursery

3 Registered childcare settings will
   a) Have limited numbers
   b) Be inspected regularly
   c) Always charge to take children
   d) Be run by volunteers

Learning Outcome 4: Understand the responsibilities of early years workers working with children

Assessment criteria grid

Learning outcomes	Assessment criteria
The learner will:	The learner can:
4 Understand the responsibilities of early years workers working with children.	4.1 Identify the responsibilities of early years workers working with children in settings.
	4.2 Describe how to prepare for working in a setting.
	4.3 Explain why it is important to know the responsibilities of own role.

4.1 Identify the responsibilities of early years workers working with children in settings

In this section we look at the responsibilities of early years workers working with children. As well as being aware of your job description or placement expectations, you need to remember a number of other key areas which we will look at:

- safeguarding
- health and safety
- working within the EYFS
- acting professionally and as a role model
- confidentiality
- awareness of policies and procedures
- managing behaviour
- understanding equality and diversity
- recognising when to refer to others
- liaising with parents/key carers.

Safeguarding and health and safety are looked at on pages 17 and 18.

Working within the EYFS

The EYFS Framework is a key document which you will need to be familiar with as an early years worker. This sets out the statutory requirements which are in three sections:

- learning and development requirements
- assessment
- safeguarding and welfare requirements.

Acting professionally and as a role model

You always need to be aware of the fact that you are a role model for the children's learning and development, and that you must act as a professional.

- Being a role model means that you should behave in a way which you would expect from others.
- Being a professional means that it should be clear to others that you are a trained and competent early years worker.

Confidentiality

Confidentiality is very important, and concerns how you treat information about children and families in your setting. We talked about this on page 89 of Unit 1. You should only discuss children and their families with other staff within the setting, and then only on a 'need to know' basis.

Awareness of policies and procedures

As we outlined in Unit 1, policies and procedures list the requirements of the setting so that staff are aware of what they should do in different situations. You need to remember that you will have to follow the setting's policies so that all staff are consistent or act in the same way.

Managing behaviour

This is another area where staff need to be consistent so that children know what to expect from all adults if they do not behave appropriately. Make sure you are clear on the procedures of the setting and what to do if you see both good and unwanted behaviour.

Test yourself

Read through the points on page 24 and answer the following:
1　What is the difference between the use of sanctions and strategies for behaviour?
2　When managing children's inappropriate behaviour, is it most important to be:
　a) friendly
　b) confident
　c) consistent?
3　What should you do if you see a child behaving well?
4　Why is your language and tone of voice important when you are managing behaviour?

Understanding equality and diversity

For more information on this, see page 26.

Test yourself

Which of these are you responsible for in an early years setting, even if you are on a placement:
- knowing about setting routines
- taking time to get to know staff
- talking to parents
- helping with record keeping
- ensuring children are kept safe
- following setting policies
- remaining professional in all situations
- knowing when to refer to others.

Recognising when to refer to others

When you are working with children, it is important that you know when to refer to others, particularly if this concerns their safety. This is particularly true of these situations:

- accidents, health and safety and safeguarding
- escalating behaviour (behaviour that appears to be getting out of control)
- use of confidential information.

However, referring to others is really the best idea in any situation when you are not sure of what to do.

For more on referring to others and the importance of your responsibilities, see pages 27–28.

For more on referring to others and the importance of your responsibilities, see pages 27–28.

Test yourself

Referring to others

- How might you know in advance what to do in the situations above?
- What is the most important reason that you should refer to others?
- Why might it be a problem if you know a child in the setting outside that environment?

Theory in action

Mariesa is on a work placement and has just had a conversation with a parent about taking a child out of the setting for a holiday: the parent has asked her about the normal setting procedure. However, as Mariesa does not know, she just tells the parent that it is fine if she does not bring her that week, and she does not need to do anything. In fact the setting policy is that parents and carers let the setting know if a child is going to be out if they know in advance.

- What should Mariesa have said to the parent as she was unsure?
- How could Mariesa have been better prepared in this situation?

Liaising with parents

The importance of liaising regularly with parents and carers is a key area of the EYFS: this is for the benefit of the children as information will be regularly passed between home and the setting. As an early years worker on placement, you should observe how more experienced staff do this with their key children so that you develop an awareness of the way this is done. If you are talking about anything confidential, or which needs to be passed to another member of staff, you should always do this as soon as possible so that action is taken.

Test yourself

Can you say whether the following statements on liaising with parents are true or false?

1 You should know the parents or carers of every child in the setting.
2 You should know the parents or carers of your key children.
3 You should greet all parents or carers every morning.
4 You should communicate face-to-face with parents and carers as much as you can.
5 You should have just as much contact with parents as other staff if you are on a placement.
6 You should let parents know immediately if there are any problems.

Test time

1 What does the term 'role model' mean?
   a) Other staff look up to you
   b) The children look up to you
   c) The parents look up to you
   d) Other students look up to you

2 Why can't you use mobile phones in childcare settings?
   a) Because you are not concentrating on what you are doing
   b) Because you might be sharing confidential information about children and families
   c) Because you have not got your hands free to help the children
   d) Because the phone might get lost

3 Why do settings have policies and procedures?
   a) Because they need to be clear about routines
   b) Because they need to be clear about health and safety
   c) Because they are helpful to refer to if there is an accident
   d) Because they are helpful for consistency in a range of situations

4.2 Describe how to prepare for working in a setting

In this section we looked at how you can prepare for working in an early years setting. Some of the things we looked at included thinking about:

- finding and communicating with a setting
- timekeeping and attendance
- dress code
- behaviour
- positive attitude
- paperwork
- DBS check.

■ Finding and communicating with a setting

In Unit 1, we thought about some of the practicalities of getting to work as well as the kind of setting you would like to work in. Depending on the amount of help you have from your school, college or training provider, you will also have to communicate with them to arrange your placement. When you are doing this, you will need to consider other issues, such as how best to approach them.

Advantages and disadvantages of different methods of communication

Method of communication	Advantages	Disadvantages
Phone		
Visiting in person		
Email or letter		

Timekeeping and attendance

When you first go to a setting, even if you are on a placement, you will want to make a good impression. In Unit 1 we talked about ways in which you can do this, particularly through your timekeeping and attendance.

Dress code

In this section we talked about making sure you dress in a way which is appropriate for the work you are doing. This is important for both practical and professional reasons.

Give two reasons why this dress would not be allowed in many early years settings

Test yourself

Can you think of two **practical** and two **professional** reasons why the correct dress is important in a childcare setting?

Behaviour

Your behaviour while you are in the setting is also very important because you are acting both as a professional and as a role model to the children. You should take your lead from other staff and make sure that you act in an appropriate way.

Test yourself

What can you do to make sure that your behaviour is appropriate for the setting? Choose three actions from the following list:

- Keep quiet when other staff are around.
- Look at what other staff do.
- Be familiar with setting policies.
- Make sure you do not 'play' with the children too much.
- Read the induction or staff handbook.
- Act as a good role model.
- Remember that you are part of the team.

Positive attitude

Having a positive attitude is important because it builds relationships with others and also shows that you are willing to support the setting in different ways.

Test yourself

Can you think of three ways you can demonstrate a positive attitude when you are in the setting?

Paperwork and DBS check

This section looked at paperwork and the DBS check. Before you start a work placement or employment in a setting, you will need to be aware of the kind of paperwork which you are expected to have. Your tutor or setting will advise you but you will need to be organised and know what you need to do. Your DBS check is particularly important. If you are on placement you will also need to keep on top of any daily paperwork which should be completed and signed.

Test yourself

What is the purpose of the DBS check? How can you make sure that you complete any necessary paperwork on time?

Test time

1 Which of the following are **not** aspects of a dress code?

   a) Tattoos and piercings

   b) Hairstyle

   c) Footwear

   d) Jewellery and make up

2 Why is your own behaviour important when working with children?

   a) Because young children do not know how to behave

   b) Because young children tend to copy adults

   c) Because young children watch you all the time

   d) Because young children cannot remember rules

3 Why is it important to have a positive attitude when working in a setting?

   a) So that others will know you are happy

   b) So that others will enjoy having you around

   c) So that others will value your contribution to the team

   d) So that others will respect you

4.3 Explain why it is important to know the responsibilities of own role

We have already talked about the responsibilities of your role on page 17. You should already be aware that some aspects of your role mean you will not always be able to make a decision in a given situation and should refer to others. This is true of anyone working in an early years setting, so it is particularly true if you are on a placement. It is important to know these responsibilities because you are acting in a professional role and need to take the children's safety into account in all situations.

You should look at the job description of an early years worker if you are not sure of your role, and be aware of setting policies and procedures and the need to be professional at all times. In section 4.1 we looked at your responsibilities regarding the aspect of children's safety. We will now think about the importance of each aspect:

- accidents, health and safety and safeguarding
- escalating behaviour
- use of confidential information
- if a child confides in you about something which has happened.

Accidents, health and safety and safeguarding

In Unit 1 we talked about what might happen if your responsibilities are not met: a key part of this is ensuring children's safety and security.

Before you start a new activity with children, give yourself a few minutes to think about the kinds of things which could be a hazard or present danger.

Why is it important to think in advance about the kinds of hazards which may occur?

Test yourself

Copy and complete Table 3.19 with some of the hazards which may occur in these situations. Add additional activities if you can.

Different hazards in early years settings

Type of activity	Potential hazard(s)	What you can do
Cooking		
Playing outside		
Walk to the park		
Water tray activity indoors		

Escalating behaviour

Another of your responsibilities is managing children's behaviour. You might find that you are in a situation where this is more than you can manage, particularly if you are on your own with children. If this happens you must always seek additional help so that children are not put in any danger.

> **Test yourself**
>
> **Escalating behaviour**
>
> Which of the following situations might you think of as escalating behaviour and seek help?
>
> - A group of older children outside who have started to have a water fight.
> - Two two-year-olds who are squabbling over a toy.
> - A six-month-old baby who has been crying for over five minutes.
> - Two four-year-old girls who have started to throw sand at each other.
> - A child who has managed to open the gate and is near the road when you are alone in the outside area with a group.

Use of confidential information

As already outlined, you must take great care if you are given confidential information about a child or family, and only pass it on to those who need to know. However, in situations where you need to, for example if the information is given to you by a parent or child, you should pass it to others in the setting straight away as it may be very important, particularly if they have confided any concerns to you.

> **Test time**
>
> 1 Why is it important to know what your responsibilities are?
>   a) Because you might have more time than other staff
>   b) Because you need to keep children safe
>   c) Because you are acting in a parental role
>   d) Because you need to gain experience
>
> 2 Why would you need to pass confidential information to others?
>   a) If it would benefit them
>   b) If it concerns their safety
>   c) If it concerns a child's safety
>   d) If a parent asks you to

■ Learning Outcome 5: Understand how to support children's development and meet their individual needs

Assessment criteria grid

| Learning outcome
The learner will: | Assessment criteria
The learner can: |
|---|---|
| 5 Understand how to support children's development and meet their individual needs. | 5.1 Identify routines and activities to safeguard the well-being of children.
5.2 Explain the importance of routines for everyday care in supporting children's development.
5.3 Identify some individual needs of children.
5.4 Describe the role of the early years worker in meeting children's individual needs.
5.5 Explain the importance of meeting children's individual needs. |

In preparation for your MCQ paper, you will need to understand how to support children's development and the role of the early years worker in meeting children's individual needs. The content for this has been looked at in both Unit 1 and Unit 2.

5.1 Identify routines and activities to safeguard the well-being of children

In order to revise for these assessment criteria, you will need to look separately at many different aspects that affect children's well-being.

Safeguarding and well-being

A good starting point is to make sure that you understand the terms 'safeguarding' and 'well-being'. Both of these terms might be used in a question.

- **Safeguarding** is about keeping children safe, which might include avoiding accidents and incidents. It can also refer to keeping children healthy.
- **Well-being** is about keeping children healthy, which includes avoiding risk of accidents. Well-being can also refer to keeping children happy.

Hygiene routines

One of the roles of the adult is to ensure that children's personal hygiene needs are met. It is important to prevent infection caused by bacteria or viruses. The term '**cross-infection**' is used when bacteria or viruses are spread from one child or adult to others.

There are several aspects to hygiene routines that we considered in Unit 2. Let's begin by looking at handwashing.

Handwashing

You will need to know the typical times when children will need to wash their hands. We looked at this on page 113. You should also be clear about the importance of handwashing in preventing infections from cross-infection. This is sometimes known as **infection control**.

Test yourself

- Make a list of times and situations when children's hands should be washed.
- Explain why handwashing is important for children's well-being.
- Do you know what the terms 'cross-infection' and 'infection control' mean?

Skin care

There are a range of activities that prevent children's skin from becoming infected and also help prevent infection from spreading. Make sure that you know what regular skin care is needed and also reasons for this.

Test yourself

- Give two examples of skin care.
- Explain why it is important for children's skin to be cared for as part of a hygiene routine.

Hair and dental care

You should also know about hair and dental care. While not all early years setting will be involved with this, you should be aware of its importance. Make sure that you know how often children's teeth should be cleaned and why hair should be regularly checked.

Test yourself

Can you decide whether these statements about personal hygiene are true or false?

1 Hands should be washed after eating.
2 Good skin care can prevent infections from spreading.
3 Children's teeth need to be cleaned every time they drink.
4 Hair care includes checking for head lice.

Many early years settings have copies of their health and safety policy online. Using an internet browser, type in the words 'health and safety policy nursery'.

- Can you find a health and safety policy?
- What types of topics are covered?

Keeping children safe

Some routines and activities are about keeping children safe. You will need to know about a range of these activities and their importance. In this section, we look in a little more detail about how to keep children safe.

Health and safety policies

Every setting has a health and safety policy. Every person working in an early years setting is responsible for knowing the policy. A health and safety policy will cover a range of procedures including what to do if:

- there is a fire or an emergency evacuation
- a child goes missing
- you notice equipment that is broken
- you are planning an outing
- there is an accident.

Risk assessment

As part of a health and safety policy, **risk assessments** will be carried out. A risk assessment is a process of identifying and preventing risks. Most settings carry out written risk assessments for activities, resources and areas that are used regularly. As well as written risk assessments, all early years workers have to be aware of potential risks at all times.

Jargon Buster

Risk assessment – a process of identifying risks and taking steps to minimise them.

Health and safety routines

There are several routines that early years workers will need to do regularly to keep children safe and healthy.

Cleaning

It is important that toys, resources and areas that children use are kept clean, including toilets. Daily cleaning is important to prevent bacteria and viruses from spreading. It is normal and good practice for indoor areas where children play to be cleaned daily, and many resources washed or wiped with disinfectant. Toys that are used by babies have to be disinfected frequently as they are likely to have been handled and put in their mouths. Other resources which children have handled or are known infection risks (such as water trays) should also be cleaned.

Food hygiene

Any area or resource that is used for food or drink has to be thoroughly cleaned. This includes tables, highchairs as well as beakers, plates and cutlery. When food is prepared, the work surfaces, chopping boards and anything being used to prepare food also have to be kept clean. There are rules in place to make sure that food is stored or cooked at correct temperatures. This is to prevent outbreaks of food poisoning.

In addition, as we have already seen, it is important that children's hands are washed before and after eating food.

Checking outdoor areas

One of the routines that early years workers need to do is to check the outdoor area before children go outdoors. This is often done without writing anything down, but it is a risk assessment. Things to check include:

- animal mess
- broken toys
- litter, for example, glass bottles
- damage to fences or gates.

Home time

To ensure that children are kept safe at home time, all early years settings will have a routine for this. Children are usually handed over to their parent or named key carer indoors or if outdoors, inside a gated area.

Activity

Create a quiz for other learners about health and safety routines.

Make sure that your quiz includes:
- the reason why personal hygiene routines are important for children
- the importance of risk assessment
- examples of everyday routines that keep children safe and healthy.

Test time

1 Personal hygiene routines are most important to
   a) Prevent infection
   b) Help children look good
   c) Help children's intellectual development
   d) Prevent children squabbling

2 Risk assessments support children's well-being by
   a) Preventing accidents and incidents
   b) Encouraging parental involvement
   c) Supporting transitions
   d) Helping children to become independent

3 What will **best** help to safeguard a child's well-being?
   a) Going for a walk
   b) Sharing a book
   c) Playing outdoors
   d) Regular hand washing

4 What is a physical need of a child aged three years?
   a) Regular outings
   b) Having a daily story
   c) Having several friends
   d) Having a balanced diet

5.2 Explain the importance of routines for everyday care in supporting children's development

As well as understanding what early years workers need to do in order to safeguard children's well-being, we also need to look at how everyday activities and routines can meet children's needs while supporting their development.

The importance of routines

It is important to be clear about the value of routines as a way of supporting children's development. We looked at this on page xx. There are two key points about routines that you should know:

- **Meeting children's needs** – routines make sure that children's basic needs are met and so support all areas of development.
- **Help children feel secure** – routines help children to feel safe as they will know what will happen. This supports their emotional development.

Test yourself

Which two of these statements are true?

1 Routines are important as a way of keeping everyone organised.
2 Routines are important to meet children's physical needs.
3 Routines are important to help children feel safe and secure.
4 Routines are important to make sure that everyone keeps on time.

Understanding children's basic needs

A good starting point is to look at pages 109–121 which looked at children's basic needs. This is because these are important when looking at routines. A good example of this is the way that children will need regular meals that are healthy.

Test yourself

Can you explain why sleep and rest, and physical activity are important for children's health and well-being?

A balanced diet including water

A healthy diet including water is one of the needs that have to be met as part of a care routine. You will need to know the importance of food for physical development, but also the importance of mealtimes for social development. We looked at this on page 111.

Test yourself

Give two reasons why a balanced diet is important for children's development.

Why are meal times an important part of routines?

Suitable clothing for the weather

You may be asked about the importance of suitable clothing as part of a routine. We looked at this on pages 112–113. Make sure that you know how appropriate clothing supports children's development.

Personal hygiene

Handwashing and care of skin, hair and teeth are part of a personal hygiene routine. You will need to know how this supports children's development. We have looked at this on pages 113–114.

Safe and secure environment

On pages 114–115 we looked at the importance of a safe and stimulating environment in meeting children's needs. Make sure that you understand how it links to children's

Test yourself

Explain the importance of appropriate clothing when it is hot and sunny.

Test yourself

Write a list of four activities associated with personal hygiene; for example, toileting.

Why is it important that this child is suitably dressed before going outdoors?

development and also how children can become involved in maintaining a safe and secure environment.

Encouraging children to be independent

One aspect of everyday care routines is to encourage children to become independent. For many of the key areas, we looked at ways in which early years workers can help children to start to become independent. You will need to read pages 116–121 carefully to find these.

> **Test yourself**
>
> Can you complete the table below using the information on pages 116–121? Some parts of it have already been completed for you.

Supporting children's independence in their care routines

Everyday care routine	What children can be encouraged to do
Mealtimes	

Learning through routines

As well as ensuring that routines meet children's needs, they can also be learning opportunities for children. We looked at some everyday activities on page 124 and considered how they might be used to support holistic development. You will need to know how different activities can be used to support children's learning.

> **Test yourself**
>
> For each of the following areas of development, explain how mealtimes can be used to promote children's learning:
>
> - physical
> - language
> - intellectual
> - social and emotional.

5.3 Identify some individual needs of children

In Unit 1 we looked at how early years workers identify children's individual needs so that they can best plan to support them in the setting. When identifying individual needs we consider:

- the child's stage of development in all areas
- any medical needs
- special educational needs
- the child's personality and interests
- the child's family and background
- any current issues affecting the child.

The child's stage of development in all areas

You will need to be familiar with the expected stages of development, such as those on pages 55–88, for children of different ages in all areas so that you have a broad knowledge of these. Alongside your working knowledge of the children themselves, you will then be able to build up a picture of whether a child is ahead, behind or in line with the expected stage of development.

Medical needs

Some children might have medical needs and conditions which you will need to know about, as well as allergies or food intolerances. These should have been identified by parents when the child starts at the setting, but they may not have been discovered. Parents and carers will also need to give the setting information about how their child's condition is usually managed. All staff should be made aware of medical needs and food intolerances; this information should be kept up to date, and all staff should know where medicines are stored.

Special educational needs

Children might have specific needs in one or more areas of learning which can impact on their development. Special educational needs is a term which is used to describe a wide range of needs, conditions or disabilities which a child may have. The younger the child, the more possibility that any special educational need has not yet come to light. Settings work with outside agencies both in identifying and working with the individual needs of each child to find how best to support them.

The child's personality and interests

As you get to know individual children, you will find out about their personality and the kinds of things which interest them. This will happen when you:

- use information forms
- observe children
- talk to them
- talk to parents and carers
- look at children's age and stage of development
- talk to colleagues about them.

How will observing children help you to find out about their interests?

The child's family background and culture

Much of the information about children's family background and culture is gathered before the child starts at the setting, through information forms which parents and carers are asked to fill in. These will include a range of information which will be confidential. However, be aware that some families might not fill in all of this information correctly, particularly if they speak English as an additional language. Always make the most of opportunities to speak to parents and carers before their child starts at the setting.

> ### Test yourself
>
> The following information will be found on a typical setting admissions form:
>
> - the child's position in their family and how many people live with them
> - the child's special educational needs
> - whether the child speaks English as an additional language
> - the name and address of the child's doctor
> - any allergies or medical conditions
> - up-to-date contact details for parents or carers.
>
> Why is each one important?

Any current issues affecting the child

Although this information on the child is important, it will also be ongoing and should be updated to ensure that the child's current needs can continue to be met. Parents and carers also need to keep the setting informed about any changes which may affect the child, although they might not always remember to do this.

> ### Theory in action
>
> Reece, three years old, has not been himself lately. From being a lively and happy boy with some friends, he has suddenly become withdrawn and has started to play on his own again.
>
> - What might you do first in this situation?
> - Why is it important that you find out whether something has happened to Reece?

> ### Test yourself
>
> Copy and complete the table on page 191, detailing how you might identify some individual needs of children.

Identifying children's individual needs

Individual need	How to identify child's individual needs
Age and stage of development in all areas	
Medical condition	
Special educational needs	
Child's personality	
Child's interests	
Family background and culture	
Current issues	

Test time

1 You need to be able to identify the individual needs of children because
   a) It is interesting
   b) Every child is different
   c) It helps to get to know them
   d) It helps you to support them better

2 Talking to children is helpful when identifying their needs because it helps to
   a) Find out about their interests
   b) Develop their speech and language skills
   c) Find out if they are okay
   d) Develop their vocabulary

5.4 Describe the role of the early years worker in meeting children's individual needs

As we saw in Unit 1, all those who work with children must plan for their needs through educational programmes which 'consider the individual needs, interests and stage of development of each child in their care' (EYFS Statutory Guidance 2014). We have already talked in section 5.3 about some of the ways we identify these needs through building a picture of each child; now we are looking at how we use this information to support their learning and development.

Ways in which we can meet children's individual needs

Early years workers can meet children's needs through:

- planning
- the key person system
- effective communication between adults.

Planning

Once we know about children's needs and interests, we can incorporate these into our planning in different ways.

Test yourself

Copy and complete the table below, showing how knowing about children's needs will enable you to plan to meet them.

Planning to meet needs

Individual need	How we plan to meet these needs
Age and stage of development in all areas	
Medical condition	
Special educational needs	
Child's personality	
Child's interests	
Family background and culture	
Current issues	

The key person system

The key person system is designed to ensure that staff get to know children and their families well, so that children can be supported more effectively in the setting.

Test yourself

Are the following statements about the key person true or false?

The key person:

1 collates information on individual children.
2 makes time to meet parents and carers every day.
3 communicates with parents and carers regularly.
4 works with the SENCO on developing EHCs.
5 passes on information to other staff when needed.
6 works with outside professionals when needed

How does the key person system help early years workers meet children's individual needs?

Effective communication between adults

All early years workers have a duty to talk to others if they have information about a child which affects them on a day-to-day basis. This may be either in the short term or long term.

Test yourself

Look at the following examples and say whether the information should be passed to another member of staff:

- A child has fallen over in the outside area and hurt her knee.
- A parent has told you that her child's pet dog has just died.
- One of the children has just moved house in the same area.
- A parent has asked you to look out for a glove which has been lost at the setting.
- One of your key children has a new baby brother and has become very tearful at drop-off time.
- A child who has had a broken arm has just come out of plaster but needs to be careful with it.

1 One of the ways early years workers can meet the individual needs of children is by
   a) Talking to them regularly
   b) Talking to parents and carers regularly
   c) Making sure they do not get upset
   d) Making sure they have a range of experiences

2 How can early years workers ensure that all staff are aware of children's medical conditions?
   a) By telling everyone about them
   b) By making sure the information is easy to find if needed
   c) By putting badges on children who have medical conditions
   d) By reminding people regularly

5.5 Explain the importance of meeting children's individual needs

It is important for early years workers to meet children's individual needs because:

- every child has an equal right to the best start in life
- it is a statutory requirement
- it personalises and enriches each child's learning.

Test yourself

Which of these policies in your setting are important when thinking about children's individual needs?

- Early Years Foundation Stage policy
- Inclusion and Equal Opportunities policy
- Health and Safety policy
- Assessment policy
- Equality and Diversity policy
- Gifted and More Able policy
- Special Educational Needs policy

Every child has an equal right to the best start in life

As we saw in Unit 1, meeting children's individual needs is important because all children need to be given equal opportunities and the chance to fulfil their own potential. One of the ways we do this is by removing any barriers to their learning. If we are not meeting each child's individual needs, we will not be giving them the opportunities they need to do this.

Barriers to learning can be caused by people's own attitudes and prejudices. Remember to use positive language and empower children by talking about what they can do, rather than what they cannot.

For more information on equal opportunities, see page 43.

Why is it important for early years workers to think about children's individual needs at all times?

Statutory requirement

The EYFS statutory guidance 2014 states that we must 'respond to each child's needs and interests' in order to guide their learning and development. You need to be aware that it is a key part of your role to make sure that you follow the EYFS guidelines so that you can meet these needs.

Activity

Read through the introduction and section 1 of the EYFS Statutory Guidance. Underline any references to the child's individual needs and how early years workers must consider them in their practice.

Check what you know

- Why does the EYFS guidance state that practitioners must think about the different ways that children learn and reflect these in their practice?
- Outline two ways in which you can respond to a child's interests. Why is this important?

Personalising and enriching each child's learning

Meeting children's individual needs effectively means that early years workers are providing a curriculum which works for each child, whatever their needs.

Test yourself

How would you plan for and meet the individual needs of:

- a child who is a refugee
- a child with significant learning needs
- a child who speaks English as a second language
- a traveller child who is new to the setting?

Test time

1 Why is it important to meet the individual needs of each child in your care?
   a) Because it helps you to get to know them
   b) Because you have to as their key person
   c) Because they all have different needs
   d) Because all children should have equal opportunities

2 Which of the following is **not** a barrier to learning?
   a) Opinions and prejudices of adults
   b) A visual impairment which is not recognised
   c) Using positive language
   d) Not including all children in an activity

3 Why must early years workers remember that each child is unique?
   a) Because this will help them to plan positive learning experiences
   b) Because children like doing different things
   c) Because workers have to cover all seven areas of learning and development
   d) Because children's needs change all the time

■ Learning Outcome 6:
Know own preferred learning style and relevant study skills

Assessment criteria grid

Learning outcomes	Assessment criteria
The learner will:	The learner can:
6 Know own preferred learning style and relevant study skills.	6.1 Explain why your own learning style is effective for you.
	6.2 Identify a range of study skills that will help you to learn.

6.1 Explain why your own learning style is effective for you

This part of the qualification looks at the way in which you learn and about your own study skills. Different theories exist about learning styles, and to begin with we looked at the main three theories which are used when describing how people learn.

Test yourself

Copy and complete the table below which defines the different learning styles. When you have finished, check with the explanation on page 45.

Can you remember your own preferred style of learning? How does this help you when organising your studies?

Extend

Research the latest theories on learning styles. What can you find out?

Different learning styles

Visual learners	
	These learners learn best through touching and doing
Auditory learners	

Finding your own learning style

Knowing your own learning style is effective because it helps you to think about how to approach your studies in a way which is beneficial for you. As well as knowing about learning styles, you will need to have an idea about what motivates you when you are learning and the way in which you approach it. These are called your **metacognitive** skills. Examples of metacognitive skills are:

- **Setting goals and planning learning** – this means being able to set small goals or targets towards what you want to achieve, so that you break your learning down into smaller chunks.
- **Monitoring learning and using strategies** – this means thinking about specific parts of your learning. It is also an effective way of managing your revision. The different strategies include:
  - Initiating your learning and being in control – make sure you do a little every day so that the prospect of an assignment or revision does not build up.
  - Self-reflect and ask yourself questions – what do I already know about this? How can I help myself to understand the information?
  - Break the learning into chunks to make it more manageable.
  - Use strategies such as mnemonics to help you – you can make these up. For example, to remember the different areas of development some people use the mnemonic, 'PILS' (physical, intellectual, language and social/emotional).
  - Checking over your work – always read through to make sure you have not missed anything.

Test yourself

Are these statements about metacognitive skills true or false?
1. It always helps to ask yourself questions about your learning.
2. Everyone finds it easier to study with a friend.
3. You should make sure you do some study every day.
4. Break your learning down, and study little and often.
5. Find strategies which work for you.

Evaluating learning

This is thinking about your learning after you have completed it, looking at it to see what you have done and whether you could have done it differently. The kinds of questions you should ask will include:

- What was I asked to do?
- Have I covered all the key questions?
- What have I learnt?
- What did I find easy/hard about the task?
- Is there anything I could change/do differently next time?

Check what you know

Think about each of the different metacognitive skills above, and write a study plan for yourself using those which will be the most useful to you.

1 When we are thinking about our learning, the most important thing to look at is

   a) How we learn best

   b) Whether we need help

   c) Whether we have taken enough notes

   d) How much time we have

2 Metacognitive skills help us to

   a) Get ready for a test

   b) Organise our learning

   c) Find out about ourselves

   d) Get our mind in the zone

3 Why might it be helpful to evaluate your learning?

   a) It reminds you what you have done

   b) It makes you do it again

   c) It makes you aware of your mistakes

   d) It makes you look closely over your work and assess it

6.2 Identify a range of study skills that will help you to learn

In Unit 1 we also looked at study skills. Knowing about and using a range of study skills is beneficial as you can find out what helps you. This includes knowing how to:

- manage your time
- find information
- make and take notes effectively
- plan an assignment
- reference and add a bibliography.

Study skills are important because they teach you to be proactive, which means taking control of your learning. You should have become aware of this and started using study skills since you looked at them in Unit 1.

How have you developed your study skills since starting your qualification?

Manage your time

You will need to think about how you make time to study for your qualification. This should be based on how you learn best and may include making the most of any quiet time that you have, or planning when to spend time studying with others.

Test yourself

Can you give two examples of how you now manage your time so that you are able to focus on your learning? What helps you to maximise the time that you have?

Find information; make and take notes

How you find, store and retrieve information when you are studying is important. You should be organised and make a note of your different sources so that you can reference them in your bibliography and acknowledge them in your written work.

Test yourself

Are these statements true or false?

1 It does not matter where you get information, as long as you acknowledge it.
2 You only need to acknowledge information if it is from a book.
3 You take notes when you listen to someone speaking, and make notes when reading through some text.
4 It helps to practise taking notes so that you can put down key points.
5 When taking notes you should not use your own words.
6 When making notes you should only write what you need.

Planning assignments

When planning your assignments, you should:

- be sure you are clear on what you are being asked to do
- read around the subject and plan your assignment carefully
- relate your research to the task.

Test yourself

Describe two ways in which you can:

- be clear on what you have been asked about
- ensure that your assignment is structured.

Test time

1 Why do you need to be serious about your study skills when you start your qualification?
   a) To maximise your time with your tutor
   b) To maximise the amount of references you use
   c) To maximise your time and keep on top of your work
   d) To maximise the credits you can get

2 What is plagiarism?
   a) Only using the book or text that you need
   b) Copying from someone else's book
   c) Not using any work but your own
   d) Sharing a book with a friend

3 Why does it help to know your own strengths and weaknesses when studying?
   a) Because you will be able to just focus on your strengths
   b) Because you will be able to just focus on your weaknesses
   c) Because you will be able to get help if you need it
   d) Because you will be able to organise your thoughts better

GLOSSARY

Anti-bias practice what the setting does to make sure that all children are treated fairly.

Assessment using observations to work out children's stage of development.

Attachment the process by which children and their parents develop a strong loving relationship.

Balanced diet the right amount and type of food that meets children's needs for growth.

Bibliography a list of books or other sources of reference.

Bonding the process by which children and their parents develop a strong loving relationship.

Confidentiality this is to do with the use of information about children and families. If you are given information which is sensitive, you must only tell others if they need to know about it.

Co-operative play where children can play together and take turns.

Cross-infection the spread of infection from one person or child to another.

DBS this stands for Disclosure and Barring Service, which was previously known as CRB or Criminal Records Bureau check. This process will check against a central register to make sure that you do not have previous criminal convictions.

Dental decay destruction of tooth enamel caused by bacteria.

Discrimination treating a person differently due to race, age, gender or disability.

Diversity understanding that each person is unique while recognising individual differences.

Early years setting an early years group where children's learning and development is nurtured by adults.

Education, health and care (EHC) plan this is a legal document which describes a child's special educational, health and social care needs. It also sets out the help that will be given to meet these needs.

Equal opportunities the right to be treated equally with others, and not discriminated against due to age, gender, race or disability.

Equality being equal, especially in terms of rights and opportunities.

Expressive language the sounds, words and sentences that babies and children can say.

Facial expressions using the face to communicate by smiling or frowning for example.

Fine motor movements small movements often made using hands such as picking up a spoon or using a pencil.

Finger foods foods that babies can eat without adult help.

Gross motor movements large movements such as running, balancing and throwing.

Head lice small insects that lay eggs and live in hair.

Holistic development children's overall development.

Inclusion making sure that all children are included in the setting through giving equal access and opportunity and removing discrimination.

Infection control steps that are taken to prevent infections from spreading.

Interaction communication that is two-way and enjoyable.

Key carer a person or people who take(s) on the role of being a child's parent.

Long term something which lasts for a longer period.

Mark-making a stage before children learn to write when they explore making marks with pens, paints and other resources.

Mentor an experienced advisor who acts as a guide and support for those who need it.

Metacognition how we think about our learning, and our own awareness and knowledge of the process so that we can evaluate it.

Milestone a significant skill that a child has mastered.

Object permanence the ability to understand that objects when placed out of sight are still in existence.

Observations noticing what children are doing and recording it, usually by writing it down.

Ofsted (Office for Standards in Education, Children's Services and Skills) Ofsted is an English government organisation which exists to monitor and inspect different types of services that care for children and young people and provide education and skills for learners of all ages.

Parallel play where children play alongside each other but not with each other.

Personal hygiene keeping skin, hair and teeth clean.

Placement co-ordinator person responsible for managing students that are on placement in the setting.

Practical comfortable and appropriate.

Prejudice assuming that you know something about a person before you know them, based on their race, age, gender or disability.

Premature this describes babies who are born earlier than expected, so are not fully developed in their mother's womb. Babies are normally considered 'full term' at 40 weeks. Twins and other multiple births may sometimes be born prematurely as there will be less space in the womb for them to develop.

Professional trained and competent.

Receptive language the words and sentences that babies and children can understand.

Resilience the ability to persist and cope when there are setbacks.

Risk assessment a process of identifying risks and taking steps to minimise them.

Role model someone who is looked up to by others as an example.

Self-settle being able to fall asleep alone without being rocked, rubbed or held by an adult.

SENCO/Area SENCO this means Special Educational Needs Co-ordinator. This person in your setting will make sure that the needs of children with SEN are being met, and will liaise with parents and professionals from outside the setting to support them.

Short term something which only lasts a short time.

Special educational needs children who have learning difficulties or a disability which makes it harder for them to learn than most children who are of the same age. This term is shortened to SEN, and is also sometimes referred to as special educational needs and disabilities (SEND).

Statutory provision for children that must be provided by law.

Strategies ways in which adults can encourage positive behaviour. For example, through verbal praise, stickers or other methods of encouragement.

Transition a change of place, family circumstance and/or of carer.

'Trial by error' learning seeing what happens after an action has been made and learning from it.

SUBJECT INDEX

Notes: Page numbers with a *b* indicate boxed material